THE
SCHOLASTIC
PROJECT

T0324096

PAST IMPERFECT

Past Imperfect presents concise critical overviews of the latest research by the world's leading scholars. Subjects cross the full range of fields in the period ca. 400—1500 CE which, in a European context, is known as the Middle Ages. Anyone interested in this period will be enthralled and enlightened by these overviews, written in provocative but accessible language. These affordable paperbacks prove that the era still retains a powerful resonance and impact throughout the world today.

Director and Editor-in-Chief

Simon Forde, *Western Michigan University*

Acquisitions Editors

Shannon Cunningham, *Milwaukee*
Ruth Kennedy, *Adelaide*

Production

Linda K. Judy, *Kalamazoo*

THE SCHOLASTIC PROJECT

Clare Monagle

Library of Congress Cataloging in Publication Data

A catalogue record for this book is available from the Library of Congress.

© **2017, Arc Humanities Press, Kalamazoo and Bradford**

ISBN 978-1-942401-07-0
e-ISBN 978-1-942401-08-7

mip-archumanitiespress.org

*This little book is devoted to the memory
of Terry Monagle, 1946–2008.*

Contents

List of Illustrations

Acknowledgements

I would like to thank the Australian Research Council for funding that supported the production of this book. I would also like to thank the Sydney Scrags for providing intellectual and emotional support. They know who they are. Many thanks to Dr. Juanita Ruys and Dr. Tomas Zahora for reading iterations of this work. Dr. Katie Chambers provided excellent research assistance. I would like to thank Professor Constant Mews for inspiration and education. Finally, I would like to thank the Modern History Department at Macquarie University for such a warm welcome, and for such generous collegial support.

Introduction

Throughout the Middle Ages, scholars in northern Europe were engaged in a project of argument, codification, and synthesis. Their task was to make a curriculum for the emerging universities that would enable students to see Christian teachings as a coherent and rational system, as something teachable. The intellectual inheritance bequeathed to these scholars encompassed the classical world, the Bible, the writings of the Church Fathers, as well as a limited range of texts written in the early Middle Ages. In addition, they had received a number of important texts via Muslim and Jewish scholars who were working in centres such as Toledo and Cairo. Medieval scholars had to reconcile this vast array of textual material with the Christian truth that they held to be absolute. Their job was to give students the benefit of the wisdom and the methods of the ancients, but always couched in the guiding knowledge of Christian revelation.[1]

The adjective "scholastic" has been used to describe this work of university-based theologians in the Latin West between approximately 1100 and 1450. They are called "scholastic" because they emerged from the cathedral schools of Europe. The *scholae* emerged during the eleventh century, concomitant to the economic and demographic renewal that took place over that century in western Europe. In places such as Paris, Chartres, and Tours, young clerics undertook training in the *trivium* (grammar, dialectic, rhetoric) as training for future careers in episcopal and secular administration. Prior to the development of the schools, higher education was conducted almost entirely in monasteries, and framed within the pedagogical objective of biblical exegesis. These flourishing towns, however, required clerics capable of ministering in an urban environment, to more fluid populations, engaged in a variety of economic activities. The intellectual program of the new schools was always intimately linked with the social transformations occurring in Europe at that time.

Their intellectual program was paradoxically timid and bold. It was timid, at least to our eyes, because these scholars were always aware of the fragility of human knowledge in a post-lapsarian world. Knowledge was always partial, as a result of the expulsion of humanity from the Garden of Eden. Yet, humans had been made in God's image, and so existed in a relationship of resemblance to God. Surely, then, this resemblance could be studied in order to learn something about God? Since God created the world, including humanity, then his creation must indicate something about his being. Medieval people knew about their separation from God, as well as their resemblance to him, through the scriptures of the Old and New Testaments. Their sense of what knowledge was possible in the world pivoted entirely upon the revelations they perceived as emerging through scripture, and was reinforced in the wisdom of the patristic fathers. Ideas that emerged from classical and Muslim worlds could be put to use, but they must always be subordinated to the truths of Christian revelation.

In order to perform this subordination, to enforce intellectual compliance, scholastic theologians employed dialectical reasoning. They placed contradictory ideas side by side, and argued towards resolving their differences and brokering orthodoxy. In the preface to his *Sic et Non*, the twelfth-century theologian Abelard (1079–1142) laid this method out in one of the earliest discussions of what came to be called "the scholastic method." In the first half of the twelfth century, he wrote:

> it seems right, as we have undertaken to collect the diverse sayings of the Holy Fathers, which stand out in our memory to some extent due to their apparent disagreement as they focus on an issue; this may lure the weaker readers to the greatest exercise of seeking the truth, and may render them sharper readers because of the investigation.[2]

The method of the schoolmen was dialectical reasoning. This way of thinking emerged from the curriculum in liberal arts in which these young men were trained, which had its origins in the classical world. They studied three core subjects: grammar, dialectic, and rhetoric. This was called the *trivium*. Grammar was the first part of their training, and constituted much more than the word signifies today. Grammar, as an area of analysis, was concerned with how language worked. As Christian theology had it, language was God-given, and enabled man's ennoblement over the beasts. Therefore, language could be read as an aspect of creation, just like the natural world. To think about a noun, then, was to think about more than a part of speech: it was also to think about what made something a thing. To say that thing was something—for example, to say, "That car is white"—invited further questions. Where does that whiteness come from? Scholars wanted to know whether every adjective—strong, pink, elaborate, wicked—corresponded to God. Grammar invited a science of correspondence, with every part of speech reflecting a higher reality.

Rhetoric was the art of persuasive speech. Again, we use a less nuanced sense of the word, often using "rhetorical" as an adjective to mean shallow or insubstantial. How often do we hear our politicians decry the "empty rhetoric" of their opponents? Within the scholastic educational system, however, rhetoric was the study of making a point, and taking your audience with you, to put it crudely. In classical Rome, rhetoric was deployed to train lawyers and orators. It was usually put to the ends of the *res publica*, or what we might call public affairs. In the European Middle Ages, however, rhetoric was put to both secular and religious ends. As a practice, it informed emerging judicial process across western Europe, as this period of educational codification was joined by one of legal consolidation. Rhetoric was also used in the production of letters, which increasingly did much of the diplomatic heavy-lifting in this period. Most importantly, however, rhetoric aided the preacher. All of the men in the schools were clerics, and many would go on to have significant careers in the clergy. Rhetoric was the structure by which they could communicate complicated theological ideas to a broader audience. Rhetoric, as a discipline, taught them when they should insert a memorable story, an *exemplum*, into their sermon, or the types of metaphors that worked best in given circumstances.

Dialectic was, put simply, training in two-fold argument. When there are two positions on any given question, how do you argue through them to find an agreement? Because scholastic theologians believed that there was an ultimate reality to which language corresponded, even if this

correspondence was cloudy, they assumed that contradic-
tions could be resolved. In fact, contradiction was a path to
the truth; the path to resolution was an opportunity to define
doctrine and to clean out problematic notions. For example,
a budding theologian in the school might be encouraged to
consider why the gospels contradicted each other at key
points. The gospels of Matthew and Luke provide different
genealogies for Joseph. Obviously, the gospels could not be
in error, as the foundational assumption for these men was
the sacredness of these texts. Therefore, working out how
they could both be true offered a way into the mechanism
of revealed truth. The budding theologian when confronted
with this problem might then think about how we should
read for allegorical or historical truth. That is, he would
find a way within human logic as he understood it to con-
trive to make it all fit. This was why scholastic theology was
highly productive if we understand "productive" to mean the
development of applied knowledge. In order to resolve con-
tradictions, theologians developed nuanced forms of literary
theory, of theories of reading, that enabled them to read for
different levels of meaning, with different burdens of proof.

A Project?

Within the discipline of Medieval Studies, scholastic thought
has been considered a method rather than a project.[3]
The reasons for this relate to the structural world of the
schools, and the universities they later became. The schools
emerged organically, rather than programmatically. They
arose with demand in the growing towns of the eleventh and
twelfth centuries, and usually responded to local need for
more clergy and ecclesiastical bureaucrats. As such, they

were completely *ad hoc*, especially when compared to the universities of today, with unit guides, learning outcomes, and standardized forms of assessment. As far as we know, and quite a lot of the early period is cloudy, a scholar would usually seek approval from the local bishop or relevant administrator to use rooms attached to the bishopric to run a class. Once approval was granted, a process that was eventually regulated to the provision of a licence to teach (*licentia docendi*), the teacher would attempt to attract students by reputation, and the students would pay the teacher directly. In the twelfth century both Abelard and John of Salisbury (ca. 1120–1180) write accounts of these schools that depict them as very loosely organized indeed.[4] They both tell the story of students following the teacher with the best reputation. They moved often, attracted by word-of-mouth recommendations. As there was no formal curriculum, and no degree structure, students were free to move as they pleased, providing they had the resources to compensate the teacher.

Perhaps because of these market forces, as we might see it, teachers defined themselves against each other. Competition was fierce for students, and so a young, up-and-coming teacher might challenge a more established figure to a disputation on a topic, an intellectual duel of sorts, in order to prove their authority. Consequently, scholastic thought itself developed dialectically, in as much as thinkers thought against each other to stake their own claims for legitimacy. This emerging theological practice, seen from a bird's-eye view, does not present as a project, but rather as a competitive practice defined by opposition. In addition, during the twelfth century a number of these schoolmen were hauled before papal councils to defend their orthodoxy. Their method was so new, and their findings so creative and seemingly counterintuitive, that the papacy was moved on a number of occasions to censure their texts, and/or restrict the verbal dissemination of their teaching. It is hard to see a homogenous project among this world of novelty and competition, one that pitted scholars against each other, and the papacy against the scholars.

The University of Paris was officially founded in 1215, although the schools of that town had been in operation for at least a century before that. The process of foundation necessitated other formal structures, such as degree structure and a set curriculum. The founding statutes of Paris set these out. During this period, universities were usually founded under the protection of the papacy or a secular ruler. They became interlocked with the establishment, as these graduates filled key administrative posts across Christendom, which was the name they gave to western Europe. It is no coincidence that the inquisition was founded at the same time, and by the same people, as those that founded the university. This was a period during which the papacy was defining its authority through the creation of new institutions that would define orthodoxy (in the case of the universities) and enforce it (in the case of the inquisition). Is it possible now to speak of scholasticism as a project, as a shared endeavour with agreed upon aims? Not really, if we think about the way these institutions operated day to day, and year to year. The universities remained highly competitive institutions, in which disputation remained one of the key means of building reputation, often at the expense of your opponents. The universities, in spite of training Europe's intelligentsia, or perhaps because they trained Europe's intelligentsia, received rigorous scrutiny from the authorities. Scholars disagreed ferociously with each other, on the page and in public. Despite attempts by Catholic historians to portray the scholastic period as a time of flowering for the Church, most recent intellectual historians of medieval thought have stressed that it was a period of competition, intellectual diversity, and creativity. In thinking of scholasticism as a method, one defined by the articulation of arguments, they have refused the totalizing vision of perfectly orthodox medieval universities. Instead contemporary scholars have shown the scholastic method as one that encouraged debate, absorbed intellectual diversity, and was often perceived with hostility by authorities.[5]

In short, much recent scholarship on scholastic theology has stressed its disruptive and contentious qualities, presenting it as an open system of inquiry, rather than a closed dogmatic structure. Scholasticism was indeed a method; I have no argument with this designation. However, it was also a project, when taken as a whole. It was a project, in as much as the Enlightenment can be conceived as such, one that depended upon a shared idea of reason as a means of coming to know the world, as well as a way of building knowledge in the world. The entry-level assumption of the scholastic project, as I am conceiving of it, is the conviction that reason is a real thing in the world (albeit God-given), and that productive knowledge of the world can best be developed by the application of reason. Anselm of Canterbury (1033–1109) argued that the world was constituted by the *ratio fidei*, the reason of faith. This was the principle that Christian faith was underscored by reason, the concepts were mutually interwoven. For Anselm, faith in a Christian God in fact enabled the apprehension of reason. Later medieval theologians understood themselves to have access to the *ordo rationis*, the order of reason, which existed as reality and was able to be apprehended by those with both the faith and the education to perceive it.[6]

The task of the scholastic project was to deploy this reason to build structures of orthodoxy in the world. Reason was used to define doctrine. Then it was was used to disseminate doctrine to believers. Reason was also used to defend the faith against its critics, both internal and external. Finally, it was used to prosecute heretics and infidels through legal argument and the creation of legal structures. Underscoring all of these endeavours, even among scholars who would have vociferously disagreed with each other in the classroom, was the idea that the practice of reason was the best guarantee of building watertight doctrine for Christendom. Reason was the gift given to humankind by God; it was in fact one of the ways humanity participated in his divinity. Reason, once given, operated independently from God, but it always bore his presence in the world.

Speaking of scholasticism as a project invariably invokes the Enlightenment as a category, and one that would seem to be the opposite of scholastic thought. Scholasticism has been commonly reviled as obscurantist and dogmatic. From the advent of humanist intellectual culture in the fifteenth century, it has been normative to relegate scholasticism as irrelevant and nonsensical. Scholasticism seems to offer the opposite of Enlightenment in fact, to be a reductive intellectual program whose purpose was to rationalize articles of faith that could not be critiqued or un-thought. For scholastic theologians, the Incarnation could never be rejected, nor the Trinity, nor the Logos. How can this foreclosed intellectual system be spoken of in the same breath as the Enlightenment, the project that proclaimed that reason enabled people to think for themselves, to transcend the verities they had taken for granted? Kant said that the motto of Enlightenment was *sapere aude*, dare to know. Given that scholastic theologians already thought they knew, we might imagine their motto was merely "dare to know how?," as they sought to defend those very verities that their Enlightenment counterparts sought to undo.

The other side of the Enlightenment project, however, are the peoples who were excluded from its regimes of reason. Through the work of postcolonial studies, in particular, we have come to understand the Enlightenment project as embedded in notions of reason to which all did not have equal purchase. The Enlightenment, it has been argued, reified a white, Western, and masculine form of reason as universal and aspirational. In so doing, Enlightenment thinkers, and the forms of governance that they inspired, produced a codified system of canonical knowledge, dogmatic in its own way. Enlightenment thought was more than a system of reasonable questions, it could be argued. Rather, Enlightenment thinkers produced an intellectual program that risked excluding forms of knowledge that could not be defended within their methodology. Within the frames of colonial and imperial practice, this enabled the rejection of ways of life, thought, and government practised by indigenous peoples on the basis that these peoples were not enlightened.

The Enlightenment project, as we conceive of it now, was much more than an injunction to know. It was a mode of thought that engendered the white Western man as the default human being, and all who were outside of that as necessarily inferior. As a mode of knowledge, the Enlightenment had emancipatory capacities, but at the same time it had the capacity to naturalize and exclude. Thinking of the Enlightenment as a project enables us to register that both things were possible in the same program, that its emancipatory and universalist ambitions sat alongside its embedded gendered, elitist, and racialized dimensions. The idea of a project enables us to attempt to come to terms with the movement as a whole. It is in this spirit that I seek to speak of a scholastic project in this book.[7]

The Reverse Side of the Project

Scholasticism was creative, disruptive, and diverse, as recent scholarship has shown us. It was also dependent on the articulation of a Western male subject, with access to reason, as the default human being, because he was made most closely in God's image. In this book I want to argue that we need to think of scholasticism as a coherent project if we are to come to terms with the constitutive work performed by this theology in the history of Western thought. Much changed between the Middle Ages and the time of Enlightenment. What did not change, however, was that the reasonable white man was the thinking subject who was allowed access to the life of the mind, and defined what it was to be reasonable. This book is the story of how scholastic theology defined this universal subject, and a catalogue of the exclusions it ensued. These exclusions still obtain today. Thinking about scholasticism as a project enables us to link the past to the present.

In what follows, I will produce a taxonomy of some of these exclusions. The categories of woman, Jew, and heretic were core others against which ideal Christian subjectivity was implicitly defined. Through their readings of Paul the Apostle, theologians mooted a putative Christian universalism in which the mechanism of baptism guaranteed equal access to salvation to all comers, be they Jews, Greeks, slaves, free, man, or woman. All Christian souls were equal before God. Life on earth, however, was a different matter. Christians lived alongside Jews. Men and women were understood to have different access to reason, and to be made in God's image in very different ways. There were always heretics who refused orthodox Christianity, as it was decreed by the papacy. Theologians used these categories as sites of investigation: how did they tell us about God's presence in the world? What epistemological and ontological purpose did these distinctions serve? In short, what work did they do? *The Scholastic Project* offers an account of this intellectual work done by categories of difference in medieval theology. In so doing, it will show just how constitutive the woman, the heretic, and the Jew were for the production of orthodoxy in the Middle Ages.

It is a more commonplace approach to look at what scholasticism has built, rather than what it excludes. Scholars have talked of a "scholastic culture," building a vision of the medieval world within which Gothic cathedrals, courtly love, and high theology are all part of the same cultural moment.[8] Within this articulation, the highest Christian ideals of universal love coalesce in new cultural forms that celebrate human flourishing through love of the divine. In thinking through the scholastic project, I seek to disaggregate the universal claims of scholasticism from the very particular forms of privilege that it inscribes. None of this is to suggest that ideas work in a vacuum, and produce their own reality. I will show, below, that the insights of scholastic theologians were produced in tandem with larger political and social shifts. The theology of Mary's Immaculate Conception evolved alongside a rise in the popular devotion to Mary.

Scholastic approaches to Jews noticeably harden alongside the increasingly persecutory regimes of Christian monarchs during the High Middle Ages. It is not always possible to work out which came first, persecutory rhetoric or practice. In this short book I am not determined to unravel that knot, but rather to demonstrate the correlations that occur between ideas, culture, and politics.

My Purpose and its Limits

I have focused primarily on three key scholastic thinkers: Peter Lombard (ca. 1096–1160), Thomas Aquinas (1225–1274), and John Duns Scotus (ca. 1265–1308). This is an inadequate sample, clearly, given the rich range of intellectuals that can nestle under the category "scholastic." However, for the purposes of this small volume, I have chosen each scholar because they are emblematic of a stage in scholastic theology, and so their comparison can tell something of a story of change over time. Lombard's epochal *Sentences* was the core textbook in theology throughout the Middle Ages. As such he is a foundational figure from the period that some call the "Twelfth-Century Renaissance." His *Sentences* constituted a core intervention during that period, transforming the new forms of theological speculation into a cogent curriculum.[9] Aquinas, of course, was the thirteenth-century author of the *Summa theologica*, the vast theological compendium that synthesized Christian theology with an Aristotelian worldview. What did this mean? It meant that Aquinas sought to understand the world of created things through the core Aristotelian idea of the *telos*, whereby everything that was found in the world was understood to be for a reason, and for an end. Aquinas wanted to understand the ends imbued within creation, and to map those ends upon an understanding of revelation.[10] Finally, I have focused upon Scotus because he had very particular things to say about Mary's Immaculate Conception, as well as the Jewish problem as he understood it. Scotus is most often considered in the light of his theory of univocity or through his arguments for the proof of God's existence. For the purposes of this book, I am interested less in his high theology, and more in how that looks when applied to doctrinal controversies on the ground.[11]

I want to be clear that this is not a survey. I am aware that the intellectual life of any period is usually more contingent and messy than any historical accounts can convey. Other scholars have done precise, meticulous, and important work on medieval thought that reveals the field as always contested. They have also shown that scholars themselves were often marginal figures, themselves prosecuted for heresy, or at least subject to censure. I am well aware that my depiction of scholastic theologians as the voices of orthodoxy does an injustice to their complicated status in the world. On the one hand, they worked in elite institutions that enjoyed the patronage of kings and popes. On the other hand, the nature of their jobs meant that they sometimes produced ideas that were displeasing to authorities, or incurred the wrath of jealous rivals. There are many moments in the history of scholastic theology where scholars were themselves maligned and marginalized. This book does not tell that story, however. My approach is to take the long view of the project, to map those categories of people who are used in the service of Christian self-definition. I have not been exhaustive in this—I could also have spoken about Muslims, lepers, or slaves as important figures in medieval theology.

When looking from twenty-first century Australia, however, it is the categories of women, heretic, and Jew that demand my attention. But this is by no means a thorough accounting. This book is a somewhat polemical, and very passionate, plea for more scholarly work that tells us not only about the house that scholasticism built, but also about those who were excluded from it.

This book is also designed for students. Firstly, I want to sketch scholastic theology as a system within which a complicated set of ideas were made to relate to each other under an overall ambition of the production of orthodoxy. Students tend to think that popes used theology instrumentally, in order to bolster their own power. Or they tend to think that theologians developed theology in order to please secular leaders. Both scenarios are too crude, and fail to register the complicated ways culture both makes and reflects reality.

Secondly, students often assume a sharp divide between the Middle Ages and modernity, seeing the Middle Ages as backward and modernity as enlightened. In telling this long story of Western othering, I hope to destabilize this narrative. The timing is right. We live in a world that is very conscious of the political realities, and implications, of entrenched privilege. We talk now of white, masculine, or heterosexual privilege. Consequently, we need to examine the history of these forms of privilege, to try to understand how they have become so embedded. That is, despite the sweeping social revolutions of recent history, we are surprised to find ourselves still living in a world where the dominant culture is patriarchal, Eurocentric, and fearful of religious others to Christianity. The reason for this dominance, I want to suggest, is the deep historical root of the idea that the universal default subject is a Western man. If we want to understand why it obtains, we need to understand deeper intellectual histories that go beyond the modern.

Thirdly, I want to suggest to students that scholastic theology was not monolithic. I hope to show how it changed over time, and that theologians of different periods took very different lines over certain things. This is not to say that it was not the discourse of elites, for elites. By this I mean that it manifested and reproduced the core interests of the ruling class, which was that of clerical men. This ruling class was ideologically invested in the masculine orthodox Christian subject as the universal human, as the measure against which all others were to be judged. As a project, scholasticism was flexible and inquiring, and creative. However, at its core it had entirely naturalized assumptions about the essential superiority of this universal *homo*. So, the project itself was highly contested and controversial in its own time, subject to censure and debate. This is not to say, however, that it did not function as a type of hegemonic soft power. I would say exactly the same thing about a myriad of intellectual movements, including those in our own day. The work of intellectuals tends to straddle the strange combination of manufacturing consent, while also producing radical critique. Scholastic theologians were no different.

Notes

[1] For background to this process, see Marcia Colish's chapter, "The Theological Enterprise," in her magisterial *Peter Lombard*, 2 vols. (Leiden: Brill, 1994), 1:33–90.

[2] Abelard, *Sic et Non*, ed. Blanche Boyer and Richard McKeon (Chicago: University of Chicago Press, 1977), Prologue, p. 103, trans. by W. J. Lewis (aided by the helpful comments and suggestions of S. Barney), published at http://sourcebooks.fordham.edu/source/Abelard-SicetNon-Prologue.asp (accessed July 5, 2016). On Abelard, see also John Marenbon, *The Philosophy of Peter Abelard* (Cambridge: Cambridge University Press, 1999), and Constant J. Mews, *The Lost Love Letters of Heloise and Abelard*, 2nd ed. (New York: Palgrave Macmillan, 2001).

[3] The classic text putting forward the idea of the scholastic method is Martin Grabmann, *Die Geschichte der scholastischen Methode*, 2 vols. (Graz: Akademische Druck- u. Verlagsanstalt, 1957; rept. of Freiburg im Breisgau: Herder, 1911). For a great introduction to debates around the definition of scholasticism, as well as to the theology itself, see Ulrich Leinsle, *Introduction to Scholastic Theology* (Washington, DC: Catholic University of America Press, 2010), trans. Michael J. Miller.

[4] John of Salisbury's account of his studies is found in his *Metalogicon*, ed. J. B Hall and K. S. B. Keats-Rohan, Corpus Christianorum continuatio mediaevalis, 98 (Turnhout: Brepols, 1991), p. 84, trans. D. McGarry, *The Metalogicon of John of Salisbury: A Twelfth-Century Defense of the Verbal and Logical Arts of the Trivium* (Berkeley: University of California Press, 1955). Abelard's story is most famously recounted in his own words in his *Historia Calamitatum*, ed. J. Monfrin (Paris: Vrin, 1978), translated in a Penguin Classics edition by Betty Radice, *The Letters of Abelard and Heloise* (Harmondsworth: Penguin, 1974).

[5] For some important recent work in the field that stresses disruption and contention, see Constance Brittain Bouchard, *"Every Valley Shall be Exalted": The Discourse of Opposites in Twelfth-Century Thought* (Ithaca: Cornell University Press, 2003); Alain Boureau, *Théologie, science et censure au XIIIe siècle: Le cas de Jean Peckham* (Paris: Belles-Lettres, 1999); and Alex J. Novikoff, *The Medieval Culture of Disputation: Pedagogy, Practice and Performance* (Philadelphia: University of Pennsylvania Press, 2013).

[6] On Anselm, see *Anselm, Aosta, Bec and Canterbury*, ed. David Luscombe and G. R. Evans (Sheffield: Sheffield Academic Press, 1996).

[7] On thinking about and through the idea of the Enlightenment project, see *What's Left of Enlightenment? A Postmodern Question*, ed. Keith Michael Baker and Peter Hans Reill (Palo Alto: Stanford University Press, 2010); *Postmodernism and the Enlightenment: New Perspectives in Eighteenth-Century French Intellectual History*, ed. Peter Gordon (New York: Routledge, 2001). On the relationship between Enlightenment thought and Postcolonial theory, see Daniel Carey and Lynn Festa, *The Postcolonial Enlightenment: Eighteenth Century Colonialism and Postcolonial Theory* (Oxford: Oxford University Press, 2013).

[8] See John W. Baldwin, *The Scholastic Culture of the Middle Ages: 1000–1300* (Long Grove, IL: Waveland, 1971).

[9] On Lombard, see Colish, *Peter Lombard*, and Philipp Rosemann, *Peter Lombard (Great Medieval Thinkers)* (Oxford: Oxford University Press, 2004).

[10] On Aquinas, see Brian Davies, *Aquinas: An Introduction* (London: Bloomsbury, 2003), and Bernard McGinn, *Thomas Aquinas's* Summa theologiae: *A Biography* (Princeton: Princeton University Press, 2014).

[11] On Scotus, see Richard Cross, *Duns Scotus (Great Medieval Thinkers)* (Oxford: Oxford University Press, 1999), and *The Cambridge Companion to Duns Scotus*, ed. Thomas Williams (Cambridge: Cambridge University Press, 2002).

Chapter 1

Woman

It is very easy to comb through scholastic sources to find those that derogate the feminine in relation to the masculine. The most famous is thirteenth-century theologian Thomas Aquinas's declaration that

> As regards the individual nature, woman is defective and misbegotten, for the active force in the male seed tends to the production of a perfect likeness in the masculine sex; while the production of woman comes from defect in the active force or from some material indisposition.[12]

This quotation embraces a range of anti-woman perceptions. It correlates action and perfection with masculinity, and it construes femininity with an always defective humanity. Most strikingly, the male seed enables a "perfect likeness," and that similitude relates to man's resemblance to God, as he was produced in his image. Women, however, as the result of a broken process, cannot participate in the same level of resemblance to God. In terms of the biological dimensions of Thomas's argument, he has embraced an Aristotelian view of generation. As a theologian, however, he has added "likeness" to the equation, making the biological ontological. In so doing, Aquinas was following his predecessor, Abelard, who had inaugurated these arguments in the century before.[13] The defectiveness of woman is no longer consigned to the realm of the earthly, but has spiritual dimensions as well. They are unable to participate in God's likeness to the same degree as men due to the imperfection of their conception.

We do not need to look hard to find more of the same within scholastic theology. Women were normatively understood to be naturally subject to men, as creatures with a lesser capacity for reason and a larger capacity for concupiscence. All souls were created equal, but souls on earth resided in bodies that were not at all equal. That is, women were as capable as men of achieving salvation. Just as for men, the criteria for their access to eternal bliss was their faith in God, their earnest participation in the sacraments, and whether or not they had lived a good and humble life. What it meant, however, to live a good and humble life on earth was not gender neutral.

Scholars who seek to recuperate scholastic theology on gender grounds stress the idea promulgated in the Middle Ages that women were as perfectible as men, but that it was a different type of perfection. Men could aspire to reason in a way that supported management of their errant wills. That is, masculinity had a privileged access to the work of the intellect. This gave the Christian man a dynamic tool for understanding his post-lapsarian desires and disciplining them appropriately. For women, it was necessarily a different capacity that oriented them to perfectibility. Their potential perfection was in subjection to their husband, be they married to a man on earth, or be they a bride of Christ. According to some interpreters, there is dignity in this difference, and ultimate equality in God's eyes.

When we extricate this male/female binary from its ontological claims, however, what remains is a complicated system of differentiation between woman and man that does conceptual work in the world. Women do not take up a lot of space in scholastic theology, yet their trace is everywhere as they constitute the idea against which the universal subject is able to be articulated. Scholastic theology is premised upon the idea of a Christian person capable of redemption through both faith and understanding. Understanding, however, was not a form of cognition to which male and female had equal purchase. Women's capacity for reason was more compromised than that of her male counterpart. In what follows in this chapter, we will explore moments in scholastic theology when this difference in capacity was articulated, and for what purposes. This is by no means an exhaustive survey; rather it constitutes a series of snapshots of the symbolic work of women in medieval theology.

Peter Lombard's *Sentences*

Peter Lombard's *Sentences* of 1156 inaugurated the architecture of scholastic thought. The work constituted Lombard's attempt to codify and synthesize his inherited intellectual tradition into a textbook for students. As the nascent schools of the early twelfth century became more numerous, and more populated with students, demand arose for better access to key ideas and texts for study. Students needed an introductory text through which they could encounter the key thinkers and the key ideas of Christian doctrine. Books were very expensive; no one but the wealthiest could develop their own library. Most students travelled from elsewhere to attend these schools. As well as having deficient means, they rarely had a stable residence where books could be stored. Students needed a foundational text that was constructed for the new pedagogical situation of the schools, and which was portable. Lombard's *Sentences* was the answer to this pedagogical challenge, and eventually became the key textbook in theological education in the Middle Ages. In fact, producing a commentary on the *Sentences* was a type of hurdle requirement over which all would-be theologians jumped in the course of their training.

In the *Sentences*, Christian doctrine was reconstituted according to Lombard's organizational schema. He was not wedded to following the order of scripture; rather he structured the information into a format appropriate for teaching. The first book focused on the Trinity, as that was the ultimate reality from which all knowledge flowed. The Trinity was that which guaranteed truth, therefore it was the first principle of cognition, it was the *sine qua non* of the entire project. In the second book, Lombard turned to Creation. In making the Trinity the subject of the first book, rather than the more obvious beginning signalled by Creation, Lombard was prioritizing doctrine over exegesis. This was a bold move. Prior to the development of the schools, most theological work occurred in monasteries and was performed in order to read the *sacra pagina*, the sacred page of scripture. The Trinity, however, was not explicitly named in scripture; as a doctrine, it emerged from theological work that extrapolated its existence from exegetical practices. Starting with the Trinity meant starting not with the sacred text, but with theology itself.

After the first two books that dealt with the Trinity and Creation, Lombard focused on the Incarnation of Christ in the third. In the Trinity he described the awesome triune

person who was ineffable and indescribable, yet also somewhat visible in the operations of creation and human history.
In describing the Creation, he detailed how humans fell and
what that meant for their souls. Book 3, on Christ, explored
the operations of saving work. Lombard went into a large
amount of detail about the constitutive parts of Christ's
being that enabled him to make reparations for the sins of
Adam and Eve. Finally, in Book 4, Lombard describes the
sacramental framework within which humans could participate in Grace. That is, after describing the enabling work of
Christ, Lombard explained how this work could be harnessed
by Christian believers to effect salvation. In both the beginning and the end of the *Sentences*, its Alpha and Omega if
you will, the emphasis was on human concepts that brought
God to man, the Trinity, and the Sacraments. In between
was the work of God, his creation, and his incarnation.

I have focused on Lombard's framework in the *Sentences*
because it is the key, I want to argue, to the architecture of
the scholastic project. Yes, the work offered a useful primer
to students about the key intellectual problems in theology.
It also, however, reconceptualized Christian doctrine away
from its scriptural roots, into a workable and teachable
system with its own coherence. In order to understand the
scholastic project, we must take stock of this foundational
move. Lombard's schema insisted on the possibility that a
theological system could be extrapolated from Christian
history, that could stand on its own on rational grounds. Of
course theologians before Lombard, the most famous being
Augustine, Anselm, and Abelard, had devoted themselves to
treatises articulating key points of Christian doctrine. What
they had not had the temerity to declare, however, was that

established doctrine could be analytically prior to the truths revealed in scripture.

Biblical Women

The move from exegesis to doctrine took a number of female biblical figures outside of the equation. When commenting on the Bible, theologians had to deal with the myriad women who appear, especially in the Hebrew Bible. Their role, both historically and archetypally, in Christian narrative needed to be understood as constitutive within the tradition. However, once doctrine had been extracted from the Bible, the discussion of "real" biblical women featured very little in theological conversations. As the object of scholastic theology was the production of doctrinal orthodoxy via dialectical negotiation, at stake was the negotiation between often abstract principles. The historical world presented by the Old and New Testaments was one of narrative and a cast of characters. A lot happened between the Alpha and the Omega. These details were of interest to scholastic theologians on the occasions that they were foundational to the revelation of truth. Unsurprisingly, the deeds of biblical women did not often figure as foundational in that way. This is not to say that scholastic theologians did not concern themselves with exegesis as a practice; exegesis remained a core scholarly task. However, I would argue that it was replaced, after the period of Peter Lombard, in scholarly privilege by the form of the treatise.

Eve and Mary were the two female figures who did feature heavily in scholastic theology. In what follows, I will explore the deployment of these figures within certain scholastic treatises, and assess the gendered implications of that work.

Eve features most heavily in scholastic articulations of the theology of will. Humans failed to will properly in the Garden of Eden. Rather than cleaving towards God, Adam and Eve indulged their desire for individuation and in so doing precipitated the fall. For Christians, then, their deformed will was the cause of human suffering and alienation. Yet, of course, the will was the way back to God. Humans must choose God freely in order to participate in the grace that facilitates redemption. In systematic Christian theology, understanding how the will worked was necessary to schematizing it as a salvific mechanism. That is, to resolve the answers to a number of questions: what was the will? How could it be oriented in the right direction? Why did it sometimes move in the wrong direction? And, generated by the Genesis story, theologians wanted to know whether men and women willed in the same way? Much ink was spilled on the last question in particular, and often the answer was given that the will of a woman was inherently more defective than that of a man. The particular reading of the Genesis story performed by medieval theologians enabled them to elaborate a theology of women's innate inferiority to men. As beings with lesser wills, they had greater capacity for sin, as well as the capacity to infect those around them with the desire to sin, such as had happened to feckless Adam (at least that is how some scholars saw it). Eve becomes the *sine qua non* of Christian history. As the agent of the fall, she established the entire world of Christian possibility. She is Christian theology's enabler in her defection from God.

Eve enabled a theory of essential female inferiority for medieval theologians. Mary enabled its opposite and a theory developed over the course of the Middle Ages regarding her utter perfection. So perfect was she considered to be that a doctrine was produced to claim that she was the result of immaculate conception, as was her son. That is, she was born without original sin, she was not subject to the sin wrought by Eve's betrayal to her God. This doctrine was highly contested among theologians throughout the Middle Ages. It was, however, considered theologically normative by 1477, when Pope Sixtus IV declared a feast day in its honour. Intellectually, what was at stake in the debates circling around Mary's status was whether God would permit his son's mother to be born in sin. In so doing, the arguments about Mary's perfection were developed within conversations about God's actions and God's desires. Concomitantly, scholars wondered whether humans could presume to know God's desires. Making Mary Immaculate required a divine intervention that could only be assumed, it could never be proven. Theologians at this late stage of scholastic theology insisted, however, that God's desires could be known in as much as it was impossible to imagine that he would not will Mary's perfection. Talking about Mary's potential perfection was also, as we shall see, a way to reconsider what could be known about God.

Deformed wills and perfected womanhood will be the subject of the remainder of this chapter. I will explore the logic by which Eve was transformed into the necessary villainess of the Christian story, and how this becomes the basis of a theology of gendered wills that obtains for all Christian subjects in the Middle Ages. The correlate of this, I will suggest, is the refusal of Mary's shared sinful humanity. The logic that produces Eve's culpability, that of her deformed will, ensures that Mary cannot be allowed to participate in that same femininity. The theology of woman that makes Eve what she is means that Mary cannot be allowed to be as she was understood to be in the early Middle Ages. She must be perfected, to avoid the stain of Eve. In narrating these intellectual moves, I will show how they generated further theological movements that had implications for other doctrines. The desire to prove a general female inferiority, and the necessary recasting of Mary as a singular woman, generated crucial theological novelty within the scholastic project.

Eve

Adam and Eve's fall is, of course, core to the Christian story. Their refusal of God's authority, which saw them banished from the Garden of Eden, is the foundational moment in the making of human subjectivity. In a post-lapsarian world, every person is born with original sin, broken and alienated. The Christian can only hope that they can be gifted with grace in order to receive the benefits of Christ's saving work. In this narrative economy, there is nothing without the fall. There is nothing to redeem, nothing to heal, there is no Omega without the Alpha. For scholastic theologians, the necessity of Adam and Eve's fall raised some challenging theological issues concerning the nature of their sin, and the relationship of their sin to God's omnipotence. In order for Adam and Eve's sin to count, for them to be culpable and therefore deserving of expulsion, they needed to will it autonomously. They had to turn away from God of their own volition. It could be argued that they were entrapped into their sin by God; or it could be argued that they were ensnared into evil by the serpent. Neither of these readings was considered possible, because they would both mean that God's punishment was both unjust and unmerciful. Since it is impossible for God to act in an imperfect way, Adam and Eve had to be understood to have sinned of their own free will and to be deserving of their banishment.

Adam and Eve, however, sinned at different stages in the story. The serpent approached Eve and promised her that she would be like a God if she ate from the tree of knowledge. Eve then, so the account goes, took the fruit to Adam, who happily joined the repast. This leads us to ask the question, was Eve more culpable than Adam because she ate the fruit because of her hubristic desire to be a God? Adam, so the exegetes argued, only ate the fruit to please Eve. Surely, then, his sin was lesser? Also, Adam and Eve's punishment was distinct. Yes, they were both banished. Eve, however, was also punished with the torment of bringing children into the world. This punishment was one that was, of course, then visited upon all women. The normative reading on the part of theologians as a result of this narrative was that yes, indeed, Eve's sin was greater, and childbirth was the gendered punishment for this lapse in judgement.

This story of Eve's particular perfidy could be sustained in individual glosses on the Book of Genesis. That is, when commenting on the biblical text in relative isolation, patristic authors could focus upon what Eve's sin meant, without worrying about its implications in other aspects of theology. When Lombard came to his systematic project, he needed to calibrate this reading of Eve, with normative theologies of will, rationality, and sin. Lombard wrote that in order for a sin to be sin it had to emerge from "the free choice of the will."[14] He defined this freedom thus: "the power of the rational soul, by which it is able to will good and evil, discerning one from the other, is called free choice."[15] One would think, then, that Eve's greater sin must be the result of her capacity for rationality. If her sin was so monumental, and the level of sin is commensurate to the degree to which it was freely chosen, then she must be highly rational in order to receive such a punishment from a just God.

In order for Eve to be the chief villain of the piece, it would seem necessary that she be accorded a high level of rationality. Sinning big, in Christian theology, required a consciously chosen departure from the right way. However, Lombard could not entertain this possibility. Rather, he tells us that she was in fact less reasonable than Adam. He writes that, "And so [the devil] tempted the woman, in whom he knew that reason was less vigorous than in the man. For his wickedness, fearful of tempting virtue, attacked human nature in that part where it seemed weaker."[16] Eve was less rational than Adam, and so the serpent chose her as the victim of his evil intentions. We would think, surely, that this lack of reason made her less culpable. She could not, presumably, choose sin adequately without access to the same degree of rationality. Yet, Lombard had no interest in mitigation for Eve. In fact, he tied himself up in his own logical knots in order to ensure that Eve's sin is registered as more profound. He writes:

> We say that Adam was not led astray in the same way as the woman: for he did not believe that what the devil said was true. And yet it may be believed that he was led astray because he thought that the offense was venial rather than deadly.[17]

Lombard's point, drawing on centuries of exegetical practice, was that Adam's sin was lesser, as he did not believe the claims the devil made for eating the fruit and he did so only to please Eve.

> But this can be so determined that we say their pride was equal in making excuses for their sin, and also in eating from

the forbidden tree; but it was unequal and much greater in the woman, in that she believed and willed to be like God, which the man did not do.[18]

Lombard argued for Eve's greater culpability repeatedly throughout the *Sentences*, even though his theology of the relationship between will and reason suggested that it ought to be otherwise.

In spite of the systematizing ambitions that Lombard declares in his book of *Sentences*, he cannot resolve this particular logical impasse. The ideological framework within which he works means that he needs Eve to be both less rational and more culpable. This is, to some degree, argumentatively unsustainable within his own theoretical terms. Yet he refused to jettison either position. The scholastic method that is being inaugurated here by Lombard isolates the two positions and shows them in sharp relief. That is, the location of theological moments when synthesis is impossible reveals the core assumptions at the heart of the enterprise. In this case, the assumption was that Eve was necessarily more guilty than Adam, even if this guilt was not necessary theologically. Lombard revealed a determination to hold on to Eve's culpability, even at the risk of his ideal of coherence.

Mary

We can therefore say that it was possible that the Blessed Virgin was not conceived in original sin. This assertion does not diminish in any way the universal redemption of her Son, as we have outlined above. We can furthermore confirm this, since the passion of Christ was immediately and principally ordered to delete original guilt as well as actual guilt, in such a way that all the Trinity, since it had the foresight of the merits of the passion of Christ, applied them to the Virgin and preserved her from all actual sin, and also from all original sin.[19]

In this statement, the theologian Duns Scotus declared that Mary's conception may well have been immaculate. The development of this Marian theology over the course of the Middle Ages also necessitated some fancy intellectual footwork on the part of theologians, what Alain Boureau has described as "spectacularly acrobatic juridical and theological speculation."[20] Producing Eve's sin as exceptional required, as we have seen, some knotty theological negotiation. The same can be said for arguments in favour of Mary's Immaculate Conception. Of course, Mary had always been special. As the mother of Christ, her position in theology had long been the subject of debate. During the patristic era, for example, some theologians debated whether saints had lived without sin. Augustine had determined that while saints may have been sinless in their deeds, they remained in the thrall of original sin as appropriate to their position as human persons. Augustine permits, however, that Mary's position in regard to sin may be anomalous.

> With the exception of the holy Virgin Mary, in whose case, out of respect for the Lord, I do not wish there to be any further question as far as sin is concerned, since how can we know what great abundance of grace was conferred on her to conquer sin in every way, seeing that she merited to conceive and bear him who certainly had no sin at all.[21]

Mary was "merited" to carry the Lord, and Augustine was clear that she must have had more than adequate grace conferred upon her in order to achieve this sacred duty. Augustine falls short of saying that she was without original sin, but he insists that her spiritual status be understood as exceptional. She was without peer among the saints.

Augustine had suggested that, "out of respect for the Lord," it was unnecessary to question Mary's status. His point was that, trusting in the Lord's logic in choosing her, she must be understood to be unimpeachable. This accommodation was unsustainable, however, during the High Middle Ages during which period scholastic theology flourished. The need to systematize theological questions, informed by the conviction that all truths could be brought together into a watertight doctrinal machine, meant that a question of such seriousness could not be left well enough alone. The problem of Mary's status was one that touched upon a number of core doctrinal issues, and so it had implications across the intellectual spectrum. There was no doubt that Mary "full of Grace" was sanctified at some point in her existence. She could not have borne Christ without being accorded a special status. But was she sanctified prior to "animation," that is, prior to conception? If this were the case, then she would no longer have been a human person according the normative understanding. Mary would be of another status altogether. Were this status to be conferred upon her, as conceived without sin, this would introduce a new category of being into the theological firmament, a being who did not require Christ's saving work to be redeemed. Ironically, the idea of Mary's Immaculate Conception perversely rendered her son's sacrifice unnecessary. If God could save a human with such ease, as in the case of Mary, why bother with the complicated drama of resurrection? Aquinas had agreed. He wrote, "If the soul of the Blessed Virgin had never incurred the stain of original sin, this would be derogatory to the dignity of Christ, by reason of his being the universal Saviour of all."[22] This was the normative position that held among theologians throughout the twelfth and thirteenth centuries. There was no need for Mary's perfect conception;

her specialness remained wholly intact without this theological escalation.

By the fourteenth century, however, Duns Scotus was arguing wholeheartedly that Mary was born without stain, that she was without *macula*. How did he make this case argumentatively? Why did he feel the need to depart from theological precedence in this way? What was at stake that justified such a repudiation of tradition? As we have seen, scholastic theology is in the thrall of its *auctoritates*. Change tends to occur via processes of systematization, rather than bald overturning. What is it about the theology of Mary's perfection that necessitated this move? There seem to be two imperatives that lead to Scotus's intellectual move. The first is that of the rise in popular devotion to the feast of the Immaculate Conception. It was a popular celebration that grew across Europe over the course of the High Middle Ages. As Marian devotion grew as a practice, it seems that there was a concomitant desire that Mary be understood as utterly exceptional, as capable of bearing a semi-divine status. The second imperative, and more relevant to this book, was that scholastic theologians had begun to theorize God's sovereign authority in a manner that departed from their predecessors. They were determined to prove that God could suspend rules whenever he so wished, as the rules were always of his own making. If God wanted Mary to have an immaculate conception, then there was no reason why he could not accord her that privilege. In this instance, the theology of Mary was a way into the theology of sovereign authority.

Mary became the exception that proved the rule, a measure of God's capacity to do whatsoever he pleases. Scotus explained that

Christ was the most perfect mediator. Therefore he exercised the highest degree of mediation in favour of another person. Now he could not be a most perfect mediator and could not repair the effects of sin to the highest degree if he did not preserve his Mother from original sin (as we shall prove). Therefore, since he was the most perfect mediator regarding the person of his Mother, from this it follows that he preserved her from original sin.[23]

Scotus's point was that since God was utterly perfect, it was argumentatively necessary that he, more particularly Christ, would do the most perfect thing for Mary. Mary was excluded from the stain as a result of a singular privilege, granted to her as a woman above all. Scotus essentially provided here the theological justification for a popular doctrine, but in so doing also articulated a model of authority that privileged the privilege as a sign of power. To make Mary immaculate, he needed to construct a God capable of suspending his own laws, and undoing his own logic. God becomes, in this telling, a sovereign authority who can make law, and undo law, in the very same moment. Mary's perfection was brokered into an articulation of the nature of power and authority.

Mary was a figure worshipped and celebrated in myriad ways across Europe during the Middle Ages. The feast of her conception, even when unofficial, was celebrated throughout Christendom. She inspired countless sermons and prayers from theologians and priests, and was deployed constantly as a figure of mediation and for emulation. She generated popular and creative fervency on the part of the lay population as well. For many scholars, the study of Marian devotion offers a way to unravel a type of theology from below. We can see the affective bonds that Christian supplicants shared with this figure via images, poetry, and prayers. As is well-known, and as is still the case today, Mary offered a site of identification and mediation. As she cradled the body of her dead son in the many iterations of the *Pietà* that were produced over the Middle Ages, Mary was instantly identifiable as profoundly human, and yet also sanctified by her proximity to the Lord. The history of Marian devotional practice offers a way into the desires and passions of believers, which often seem far removed from the complicated arguments of theologians.

The debates about Mary's Immaculate Conception, however, bring the realm of the affective together with that of high theology. Mary's exceptional status in theology, as the one human person to receive the privilege of an immaculate conception, may have been suggested or sought through devotional practices. It became doctrinal, however, through argument. The *Salve Regina*, below, had been sung since the eleventh century, and its performance was a commonplace in liturgical practice. The prayer reads:

> Hail, holy Queen, Mother of Mercy,
> Hail, our life, our sweetness and our hope.
> To thee do we cry,
> Poor banished children of Eve;
> To thee do we send up our sighs,
> Mourning and weeping in this valley of tears.[24]

This text is but one example of the necessity of Mary to the Christian imaginary. She is the corollary of Eve, the mother who nurtures the wounds of the fall. The theory of the Immaculate Conception, as expressed by Scotus and others, amplified and reified this devotional role. They did so not in recognition of the power of the feminine, however, but in order to reveal God's extraordinary capacities as sovereign. That is, Mary's perfection was not warranted by her deeds, but given to her as a privilege.

Conclusion

Eve and Mary perform conceptual work in scholastic theology. Lombard developed a theory of Eve's sin that combines a telling of both her excessive irrationality and her excessive sin. Lombard argued elsewhere that the best measure of the degree of sin was the level of reason of the sinner. That is, the greater the capacity the sinner had to choose their sin in a rational manner, the graver their error was considered to be. Yet Lombard repudiated his own logic to explain Eve's culpability, arguing that her very lack of reason rendered her more vulnerable to the advances of the serpent, and thus worse than Adam. In doing this, Lombard pathologized the woman as innately and intimately driven to sin, without having any of the reason that would enable her to detect her own inclinations to error. It is a damning and intractable view that essentialized the feminine, and reduces women's capacity for transformation through reason. At the other end of the scholastic project, Scotus told a story of feminine perfectibility that is understood as being entirely exceptional. Mary was increasingly inscribed as a site of the most perfect purity, but one that can only occur as the result of privilege, rather than merit. The theology of the Immaculate Conception, ironically, reduced the importance of Mary's personhood. It made the discourse about Mary all about, instead, God's extraordinary powers. It was not so much that Mary merited her status, but rather that God accorded it to her in an act of sovereignty.

In both of these cases, we see the capacity of scholastic thought to harden categories. Scholastic methods sought to settle doctrinal issues, and to consolidate plurality into synthesis. As we shall see in the following chapter, this method was enabling in certain ways. It enabled the production of institutional coherence as well as forms of legal codification that aided in the administration of growing populations and the development of systems of justice and education. In so doing, however, hierarchies were written into the system that privileged certain forms of being. The examples of both Eve and Mary show the degree to which the two major female figures in the tradition were instrumentalized in the making of doctrine. In Eve's case, she was refused mitigation by Lombard, even when he understood her to be without adequate reason to sin properly. In Mary's case, her earned perfection was jettisoned in favour of her wholly exceptional perfection, granted to her by God. Lombard's theology abjected Eve, amplifying her bestial humanity at the expense of her reason. Scotus's theology celebrated Mary's purity, but removed her agency in the attainment of her special status.

Notes

[12] Thomas Aquinas, *Summa theologiae* I.92.i.i, trans. Laurence Shapcote, ed. and rev. the Aquinas Institute and its collaborators (Lander: Aquinas Institute for the Study of Sacred Doctrine, 2012), p. 416. The *Summa theologiae* (also known as the *Summa theologica*) is divided into three parts, the second of which is itself divided into two parts (which is shown below as II-I or II-II. Each of these parts has a series of numbered questions dealing with major theological issues. The questions are often subdivided into particular problems, called articles, and these are then debated with arguments in favour and against. So, "I.92.i.i" means that it relates to part I, question 92 (on the production of woman by God), the first article ("on whether woman should have been made in that first production of things [on earth, during creation]"), and this is the response ["i"] to the first argument on this article.

[13] On the theological precedents for Aquinas's theology of women, see Juanita Ruys, "Ut sexu sic animo: The Resolution of Sex and Gender in the *Planctus* of Abelard," *Medium Aevum* 75 (2006): 2–23.

[14] Peter Lombard, *The Sentences* 2.22.5.3, trans. Giulio Silano as *The Sentences Book 2: On Creation* (Toronto: Pontifical Institute of Mediaeval Studies, 2009), p. 103. Lombard's *Sentences* is in four volumes, and is divided after that into distinctions, then chapters, then notes.

[15] Lombard, *The Sentences* 2.24.3.1, p. 109.

[16] Lombard, *The Sentences* 2.21.1.2, p. 92.

[17] Lombard, *The Sentences* 2.22.3.2, p. 99.

[18] Lombard, *The Sentences* 2.22.4.6, p. 101.

[19] John Duns Scotus, *Opera Omnia: Lectura in librum tertium Sententiarum. Distinctiones* 1-17 (Vatican City: Typis Polyglattis Vaticanis, 2003), 20:138.

[20] Alain Boureau, "Privilege in Medieval Societies from the Twelfth to the Fourteenth Century: or, How the Exception Proves the Rule," in *The Medieval World*, ed. Janet Nelson and Peter Linehan (Abingdon: Routledge, 2001), pp. 621–34 at 630.

[21] Augustine, *De natura et gratia, Patrologia cursus completus, series latina* (=Patrologia Latina), 221 vols. (Paris: Migne, 1844–1902), vol. 44 (1865), col. 267. Quoted in Sarah Jane Boss, *Mary: The Complete Resource* (London: Bloomsbury, 2007), p. 100.

[22] *Summa theologiae* III.27.ii.ii, p. 285.

[23] Scotus, *Lectura in librum tertium*, p. 123.

[24] See Miri Rubin, *The Meaning of Mary in Medieval Religious Cultures* (Budapest: Central European University Press, 2009).

Chapter 2

The Heretic

A heretic is one who turns away from orthodoxy, from correct teaching. Normally defined, a heretic obdurately clings to their own ideas about the right path, even when it contradicts established authority and canonical texts. A heresy can only be said to exist when it can be contrasted against a norm. Without a norm against which it can be defined, heresy is simply a set of beliefs, a mode of worship, or a ritual practice. My point is that heresy never simply is, but needs to be categorized and defined in order to exist. It is no wonder, then, that the rise of scholastic theology coincided with what R. I. Moore famously argued was the development of the "persecuting society" in the Latin West.[25] The period of the High Middle Ages saw the codification of law and theology, in which previously unwritten or diffuse laws and ideas were transformed into bounded systems of knowledge. In so doing the division between heresy and orthodoxy, or between criminality and legality, became much starker. The persecuting society, as defined by Moore, was one where authorities deployed these new definitions of orthodoxy in order to divide populations between the saved and the unsaved, the faithful and the deviant. In this way, Moore argued persuasively, authorities could bolster their own authority by defining an other against which the Christian subject could be defined. As we still see today, the demonization of difference enables the production of a political imaginary that privileges purity and righteousness. It was no different in the Middle Ages.

Paul wrote to the Corinthians, "For there must be also heresies: that they which are approved, may be made manifest among you" (1. Cor. 11:19). The demarcation of heresy was necessary to the making of Christian orthodoxy. The heretic, in fact, enabled the definition of the faithful. From the beginning of Christianity, doctrines were formulated and refined through processes of argument and contestation. Most notably, core aspects of both Trinitarian and Incarnational theology were established in the period between 100 and 450 CE. The process of making doctrine was one in which some forms of Christian worship and belief were declared orthodox, and some were demarcated as erroneous. During the Patristic era there were myriad christianities, with a likewise myriad set of beliefs, devotional practices, and rituals. As Christianity gained in prestige and institutional clout, it was considered necessary by religious and secular authorities that these various forms of worship and theologies be defined more tightly into an orthodoxy, that is, a set of correct and endorsed teachings. In order to do this, ecumenical councils were convened by the emperor. Ecumenical councils brought together theologians and ecclesiastical elites. Such councils were considered to be ecumenical because their brief was the entirety of the Christian world. They received delegates across the diverse locations of Christian worship.

These councils were often prompted by diversity of beliefs that were troubling, in one way or another, to Christian order. For example, the most famous ecumenical council of the patristic era was that of Nicaea, convened by Constantine in 325 CE. This council was called to respond to Arius, a theologian who had argued that God the Father must be considered to be in distinction from Christ the Son, as the former had produced the latter from non-existence. Therefore, they could not be understood to be the same person, as one had existed without the other. This argument was in contradiction with normative, if emerging, trinitarian theology that held that the Father, the Son, and the Holy Spirit were three-in-one—the three persons of the triune God. Arius held strong support for his views in pockets of the Christian world, and Constantine was concerned enough by the disruptive force of this argument that he convened a council to resolve the issue. At stake, of course, were not only the intricacies of the Trinity, but the question of the necessity of a centralized form of orthodoxy. Constantine's newly christianized empire required consistency of observance and doctrine. In order to counter Arius's ideas, the Council produced the Nicene Creed. This was a statement, endorsed by the Council, that declared the essence of Christian belief. The text read, in part,

> I believe in one God, the Father Almighty, maker of heaven and earth and of all things visible and invisible.
>
> And in one Lord Jesus Christ, the only-begotten Son of God, begotten of the Father before all worlds; God of God, Light of Light, very God of very God; begotten not made, being of one substance [homoousios] with the Father, by whom all things were made.[26]

The Nicene Creed, once established, then became a yardstick for orthodoxy against which theological claims could be assessed.

To define orthodoxy at Nicaea, however, required the introduction of this Greek word *homoousios*. This word was used to explain the co-substantiality of the Son and the Father. In short, it was a technical word used to describe their utter identity to each other, their sameness. This word was not taken from the Bible. Rather, it was injected into theology in order to solve a problem introduced by dissension and critique. Arius had asked how it was possible that God and Christ be one and the same, given that one generated the other. *Homoousios* provided the conceptual response; the Council of Nicaea deployed a theological novelty in order to define their orthodoxy. In so doing, the Council established a type of inviolable theological precedence within which subsequent theologians would have to negotiate their positions. Orthodoxy was never simply a given, but always a process of negotiation and contestation. This one example goes some way to show the means by which theological novelty was produced during the patristic era, and then also in the High Middle Ages. Theology developed over time as a result, mostly, of conflict, argument, and challenge. A solution, such as *homoousios*, emerged as a way to broker difference, and to assert authority. This is the process through which heresy was defined—it was the correlate of this refining of doctrinal lines. Arius and his supporters were not heretics until their theology was declared in error by the councils. Prior to the councils, they were Christians with questions.[27]

This example helps explain the importance of theological language in the definition of heresy. All too often the word "heretic" conjures images of the individual in flagrant and determined rebellion against ecclesiastical authorities. In modernity, we tend to respect the heretic as the person who speaks the truth to corrupt and ignorant authorities. The prosecution of Galileo for heresy, for example, would seem to situate the divide in those terms. What I want to talk about in this chapter, however, is less dramatic or clichéd. For what we see in the Middle Ages is a series of processes not dissimilar to Nicaea, whereby changing theological definitions produce new heresy. Although the behaviour and beliefs of populations may not necessarily change, how they are understood and defined by authorities does. In what follows, I want to consider how the work of the scholastic project to build an edifice of doctrine invariably produced heresies, in as much as theologians attempted to codify what it was to be a proper member of Christendom. In so doing, there were inevitable exclusions.

This is not to say that scholastic theologians were inquisitors. They did not police or prosecute heresy. Rather, it is to show how the articulation of orthodoxy and heresy as categories was foundational to the work done by theologians. To do theology was to produce the boundaries around licit and illicit God-talk. It was to say what was true, and what was false. To do theology was to explain what could be understood, and what was beyond human conceptions. The concept of heresy itself was integral to that intellectual process; heresies were necessary in order that the righteous be manifest. There could not be orthodoxy without its outside, at least according to the Pauline formulation.

The Fourth Lateran Council of 1215

Lateran IV was the most important papal council of the High Middle Ages.[28] It was important because it generated a bold and ambitious program of papal legislation. Among the items covered by the constitutions of Lateran IV was the call for a new crusade, the mandating of yearly confession, the banning of clerical oversight of ordeals, and the stipulation that Jews and Muslims wear identifying clothing in Christian communities. It proposed the boldest set of reforms of any council in the Middle Ages, and represents the medieval papacy's most ambitious moment. The scale and the program of Lateran IV harked back to the great councils of the patristic era, and attempted to revitalize the papal councils as a political organ. During the fractured period of the early Middle Ages, the councils had fallen into abeyance as an important structure of governance within Europe. Its revival from the eleventh century was one register, among many, of increasing stability and confidence across the continent. This confidence was expressed in the statement of faith with which Canon 1 of the Council began.

> We firmly believe and simply confess that there is only one true God, eternal and immeasurable, almighty, unchangeable, incomprehensible and ineffable, Father, Son and holy Spirit; three Persons but one absolutely simple essence substance, or nature; the Father is from none, the Son from the Father alone, and the holy Spirit from both equally, eternally without beginning and end.[29]

This may seem formulaic, but by starting with a declaration of faith, the Fourth Lateran Council declared itself to be in the foundational tradition of the great ecumenical councils in the past. Other councils during the preceding centuries had been reactive; they had usually concerned themselves with particular issues from the outset. This council, however, began with a very precise statement of the core tenets of Christian belief.

Pope Innocent III oversaw this council, and he was the first pope who had been trained in the schools. That is, he was the first pope to receive training in this new dialectical approach to theological problems that was being developed, and promulgated, in the schools of northern Europe. The then Lothar de Segni had spent some time in the 1170s or 1180s training in Paris. Innocent III's intellectual formation occurred in a post-*Sentences* context. He was educated by the generation of scholars who followed Lombard, scholars who were keen to apply his methodology to a large array of pastoral and sacramental issues. By the time the future pope was taking his theological education, the scholastic approach was being applied not only to high theology, but to thinking through the broad range of issues that obtained in ecclesiastical administration. These were questions such as how penance should be apportioned fairly, or what it meant when an ecclesiastical authority placed a secular leader under interdict. Innocent III's intellectual formation, then, occurred in the context of early scholastic culture. This was a culture that prized disputation and dialectic as a means not only to negotiate problems, but also to arrive at demonstrable and stable truth.

Innocent III surrounded himself with schoolmen as key advisors and administrators. In particular, he appointed two eminent Paris-based theologians as cardinals, Robert of Courson and Stephen Langton. Customarily, cardinals had tended to be Italian-born and to come from leading aristocratic families with proximity to the Vatican. These men were entrusted with much of the preliminary work for the Council, such as building support for the endeavour throughout Christendom, as well as setting the agenda for the work of the Council. Their involvement matters, as does that of Innocent, because Lateran IV was the emblematic council of the so-called persecuting society. This was the Council that firmly declared papal sovereignty over Christendom, enshrining the right of the Church to define the border between heretic and saved. The council declared, "There is indeed one universal church of the faithful, outside of which nobody at all is saved," in so doing asserting a claim to hold a complete monopoly over orthodoxy.[30]

The centrality of scholastic theology to the project of the Council was evinced in the startling endorsement of Peter Lombard within the constitutions of the Council. The first canon, as we have seen, was devoted to a *credo*, a particularly bold confession of faith. The second canon condemned ideas found within a book written by the controversial abbot Joachim of Fiore. In a book that is unfortunately no longer extant, Joachim had apparently accused Lombard of heresy in regards to the Trinity. Lombard, Joachim alleged, had turned the Trinity into a heretical quaternity because he said that there was a common essence that united the three persons, which explained their one-ness. Although Joachim had himself died in 1202, his name remained a byword for an approach to exegesis that was analogical and apocalyptic. Joachim was a popular preacher and self-styled prophet, who claimed to be able to unravel arcane mysteries in order to map out the end of times. Joachim's popular appeal lay in his spiritualism and futurology. As much as we can guess, Joachim's critique of Lombard would have betrayed scepticism against the approach of the author of the *Sentences* (and other schoolmen) to divine mysteries. Joachim understood sacred mystery as sites for contemplation through which mystical insight could be gained. For the schoolmen, mystery was a site for explication and understanding—*fides quaerens intellectum* (faith seeking understanding), as the eleventh-century theologian Anselm of Canterbury had described it. Mapping the contours of a doctrine as elusive as the Trinity or the Incarnation offered scholastic theologians a roadmap to learn more about God and the world that he created. They aimed to create usable knowledge. Joachim, on the other hand, worked in a prophetic mode. When Lombard looked at the three persons of the Trinity, he sought to name that ineffable thing that constituted their unity. Joachim, according to the Council, felt that such a definition violated divine mystery, and reduced God's dignity.[31]

We must always be wary of creating a false distinction between monastic and scholastic knowledge. One of the most clichéd images of medieval intellectual life is that of proto-modern university scholars in battle with conservative monastic scholars. The story of Abelard and Bernard of Clairvaux, for example, is often still told in this way, with rational Abelard being called to account by a judgemental and conniving Bernard. The story of relationships on the ground, however, between monks and schoolmen was often much more complicated. Yes, Bernard of Clairvaux mounted prosecutions against two of the most prominent schoolmen of his day, Abelard and Gilbert of Poitiers. At the same time, he acted as a patron to a number of schoolmen. In fact, he wrote a letter of recommendation for Peter Lombard early in the theologian's career. In the relatively small intellectual contexts of northern Europe in the twelfth and early thirteenth centuries there was significant institutional and social overlap between the monastic and scholastic sector.

Yet in spite of this overlap, Joachim and Lombard were set up as opponents in Canon 2 of Lateran IV. The monk and the schoolman were placed in clear juxtaposition. The Council records Joachim's criticisms of Lombard, and reprises the charge that Lombard had created a quaternity. Then, the

Council leapt to the defence of Lombard, declaring that it sided *cum Petro*.

> We, however, with the approval of this sacred and universal Council, believe and confess with Peter that there exists a certain supreme reality (res), incomprehensible and ineffable, which truly is the Father and the Son and the holy Spirit, the three persons together and each one of them separately. Therefore in God there is only a Trinity, not a quaternity, since each of the three persons is that reality—that is to say substance, essence or divine nature—which alone is the principle of all things, besides which no other principle can be found.[32]

In fact, the Council not only endorsed Lombard's orthodoxy generally, but they agreed that it was appropriate to define *una quaedam summa res* (a certain highest reality), in order to put a name to the unity of the Trinity. This unity was understood to be beyond human conception, completely total, and perfect. Against Joachim's point that this mystery was to be revered rather than interrogated, the Council declared that Lombard's analysis and naming was adequate to the mystery, if not identical, with it. In so doing, as I have argued elsewhere, the Council endorsed the scholastic method. In the most prestigious of locations, in the most binding of language, the constitutions of Lateran IV aligned themselves firmly *cum Petro* and *contra Joachim*. Finally, the constitutions decreed that anyone who supported Joachim on this point should be "repressed by all as a heretic."[33]

It was unprecedented to elevate a contemporary theologian in this way. Why would the Council be moved to do this? What is the relationship between the intricacies of Trinitarian theology and the broad agenda of the Council? My answer is that the scholastic project was instrumental to the work that the papacy wanted to achieve in Lateran IV. In fact, at that historical moment, I suggest that the lines between scholastic theologians and the institution of the papacy were very blurry indeed. The papacy and the schoolmen were both engaged in acts of inscription and definition. The work of theology was to draw borders around Christian truth, to make clear what could and could not be said, and what could and could not be known. The work of the papacy, as this bold pope understood it, was to demarcate the ideological borders of Christendom, to work out who was inside and who was out. The remainder of the statutes of Lateran IV worked at these definitions, at prescribing the forms of worship, modes of practice, and set of doctrines that guaranteed inclusion and salvation. Lombard's endorsement preceded this work, and arrived just after a confession of faith. The persecuting society and the scholastic project, at least at this moment, were moving together.

There are a number of other indicators in the language of Lateran IV as to the mutuality of the papacy and the schoolmen at this time. This is not the place to go through all of them. But it is important to note that it is in the canons of Lateran IV that we see the first official use of the term "transubstantiation" to describe the changes that occur within the host as part of the Sacrament of the Eucharist. Lateran IV, thus, was not only used to mandate events such as crusades and to regularize confession, it was also used to sanction a neologism. Just as the deployment of *homoousios* was one of the outcomes of Nicaea, so the strategic use of "transubstantiation" was one of the innovations of Lateran IV. Throughout the eleventh and twelfth centuries there had been much debate about the nature of the transformation of the bread and wine that occurred. The question was whether or not the change that occurred was "real," that is, was there a genuine change to the bread and wine as a result of consecration? When the priest said, "This is my body," was the bread actually Christ's body, despite appearing unchanged? Or was the shift only spiritual? Was the bread infused with grace, but still fundamentally bread? This question might seem absurd to our eyes: if it looks and tastes like bread, then surely it remains bread in some basic, fundamental way. We have been trained to trust our physical interactions with the world as a source for veracity. During the Middle Ages, however, the question of the Eucharist challenged such assumptions. Ought we trust our experience? The bread may be entirely bread-like, but this does not mean that it cannot also be utterly the Body of Christ at the same time. Like the unity of the Trinity, this change was ultimately only comprehended through faith, rather than reason. The Council deployed the word "transubstantiation' to name this mystery precisely. The word was a container for this paradox, between the physical reality of the bread and the spiritual reality that it was the Body of Christ. "Transubstantiation" was the name for this in-between.

The University of Paris

Lateran IV in 1215, then, licensed theologians to define mystery, and accordingly to redefine orthodoxy. As an event, it is of fundamental importance to the scholastic project as it reveals the centrality of scholastic ideas to the workings of the papacy. In that same year, Innocent's legate Robert of Courson was also charged with writing the founding statutes for the University of Paris. This university had been established formally by King Philip Augustus in 1200, but was only ratified by the papacy in 1215. The university statutes legislated the ages by which a scholar could be authorized to lecture in the Arts, as well as in the Faculty of Theology. It laid down a series of rules to govern the operations of the university, prescribing core texts, as well as more mundane administrative matters. Most crucially, the statutes made clear that the breaching of these rules was a serious matter, and finished with the following warning:

> In order moreover that these may be inviolably observed, all who presume contumaciously to violate these our statutes, unless within fifteen days from the date of the transgression take care, to correct their presumption in the presence of the university masters and scholars, or in the presence of some appointed by the university, by the authority of the legation with which we are entrusted, we bind with the bond of excommunication.[34]

The stakes for this new institution were high, and its responsibilities were serious. Hence, to be in breach was to be excluded entirely from the Christian order. This was the new world order of the thirteenth century, one that opposed orthodoxy to heresy in clear binary terms. Little mercy could be shown: if the plaintiff refused to seek mitigation through correction and remorse, they paid the highest of prices.

This type of punishment, ironically, mirrored the punishment declared in the canons of Lateran IV for all heretics. Canon 3 decreed that

> We excommunicate and anathematize every heresy raising itself up against this holy, orthodox and Catholic faith which we have expounded above; we condemn all heretics, whatever names they may go under. They have different faces but their tails are tied together inasmuch as they are alike in their pride.[35]

As we have seen, Canon 1 of Lateran IV made a declaration of faith, one that included transubstantiation for the first time.

Canon 2 of Lateran IV endorsed Peter Lombard as orthodox, whilst explicating and approving his trinitarian theology. Canon 3 boldly performed a mass, albeit abstract, excommunication that in its temporal generality seemed to speak to every heretic, present and future. Taken together, these three canons produce a rigid dichotomy between the holy, orthodox, and Catholic faith, and the heresies that refuse that faith. Scholastic theology provided the core theological doctrines against which the heretic could be judged. They built the orthodoxy, and in so doing condemned those who fell beyond its borders.

The Figure of the Heretic

The work of policing heresy, of administering "the persecuting society," fell not to theologians, but to inquisitors. The history of the inquisition as an institution, and as a process, has been told elsewhere, and is not the subject of this book. It is important, however, that we understand that inquisitors could not have done their work without a well-articulated construction of the idea of the heretic. Historiographical debates concerned with heresy in the Middle Ages have focused upon a core question. Can we talk about "real" heretics, and write their history? Or does heresy only exist in the Middle Ages as a category invented by elites? Are heretics, as they were defined at the time, people who fell on the wrong side of a set of theological definitions? Or were they heretics proper, in as much as they can be constituted as groups of people who deliberately and self-consciously rejected the authority of the Church, as well as core doctrines? Wherever the answer falls, it is clear that the concept of the heretic was one of the core conceptual tools that ecclesiastical leaders and scholastic theologians had at their disposal to think through the idea of what was legitimate and what was not.

Thomas Aquinas was, and is, the most famous, and most influential, of all scholastic theologians. In the remainder of this chapter, I will explore his understanding of the heretic. Aquinas, the so-called "Angelic Doctor," has long dominated our understanding of medieval thought. In the narrative promoted by his disciples to this day, Aquinas famously combined Aristotelian and Christian learning into a detailed, sophisticated, and architectonic synthesis. He devised a framework within which the bountiful insights into natural philosophy, literature, politics, and logic offered by an immersion in the works of Aristotle could be combined within a Christian eschatology and anthropology. He took Aristotle's insights into the ways of the world and integrated them with Christian understandings of the ways of God. In this view, prior to Aquinas, Christian thinkers had been concerned primarily with interpreting sacred texts to build moral and spiritual schemas. Although they deployed the methods of argumentation and literary analysis they found within the classical tradition to read and understand Christian sources, their final objectives tended to be either mystical union with God or the elaboration of doctrine. Aquinas, so the story goes, was interested in a much bigger picture. As well as being concerned with the articulation of spiritual truths, he was also concerned to understand the logic of the world, to deploy sensory experience of the lived world in order to understand human behaviour and the physical world. The fruits of Aquinas's synthetic genius can be found in his exhaustive *Summa theologiae*, the massive compendium of his lifetime's investigation in Christian theology and classical learning, written between 1265 and 1274.

Aquinas was interested in all aspects of Christian life. For example, unlike previous scholars working in the scholastic framework, he devoted significant attention to the role that the *passiones animae*, the passions of the soul, played in human subjectivity. The passions of the soul corresponded to what we, today, call the emotions. Prior to Aquinas, emotions had tended to be understood as bodily feelings that had the potential to disrupt the good Christian life, locating the individual too much in worldly life, as opposed to orienting them to the divine. Aquinas, however, argued that emotions were a core aspect of what it was to be human, and therefore necessitated analysis and understanding. As humans were made in God's image, and as Christ himself had been human, it was understood that building a nuanced understanding of the Christian person was theological work.

Aquinas understood the human person as a complicated psychosomatic creature who experienced myriad feelings and desires. For Aquinas, his scholastic project was to use taxonomies and definitions to better understand the complicated terrain of the human. How could the multiple components that constituted the human be understood in relationship to Christian revelation and to salvation? For Aquinas, then, heresy threatened to contaminate Christians; it threatened the very delicate ecosystem that enabled Christian belief to flourish. When writing about heresy, as the scholastic method entailed, Aquinas quoted previous authorities, and reprised already well-known positions. My argument here, however, is that his seemingly formulaic pronouncements on the contagion of heresy should be read as urgent in light of his anthropology of the human person, whose orientation to God must be embodied, willed, and felt, as well as understood rationally. Aquinas says that

> heresy and sect are the same thing, and each belongs to the work of the flesh, not indeed by reason of the act itself of unbelief in respect of its proximate object, but by reason of its cause, which is either desire of an undue end in which way it arises from pride or covetousness, as stated in the second objection, or some illusion of the imagination.[36]

Here, he analysed heresy from a psychosomatic perspective, ascertaining which part of the sin is bodily, as opposed to intellectual. He suggests that heresy or sectarianism, both of which mean a cutting off, are embodied in as much as they derive from pride and covetousness, or from irrational illusion. Heresy occurs when these bodily processes produce a refusal of orthodoxy, when they fixate upon erroneous ideas in the mistaken belief that these ideas will satisfy carnal feelings. The heretical idea, then, cannot be divested from the heretic. The capacity of the person to project upon error, and to enjoy it, is not merely a question of thinking wrongly; it is also an indication of warped and broken patterns of feeling.

This means that the danger posed by the heretic cannot be limited to a conceptual error that can be abjured and be done with. Rather, once an individual has allowed themselves to be deceived by heresy, they have shown themselves to be disposed towards it at a deep somatic level. In order to show the risk that these deformed individuals pose, he quoted Jerome on the threat to the Christian community,

> Cut off the decayed flesh, expel the mangy sheep from the fold, lest the whole house, the whole paste, the whole body, the whole flock, burn, perish, rot, die. Arius was but one spark in Alexandria, but as that spark was not at once put out, the whole earth was laid waste to its flame.[37]

The quotation from Jerome enabled Aquinas to refer back to the Arian controversy, which as we saw earlier was the subject of the Council of Nicaea. Heresy contaminates and spreads, and it is worth the sacrifice of the individual to save the community. Aquinas was reminding his readers that the management of heresy is an ongoing, if not eternal, struggle, and that constant vigilance is required. In addition, Aquinas fortified this theology with his insistence that the heretic be given little opportunity to repent, in spite of the theological imperative to mercy of which he is fully aware. He writes that they will be given one chance at returning to the faith, but one chance only: "But when they fall again, after having been received, this seems to prove them as being inconstant in faith, wherefore when they return again, they are admitted to Penance, but are not removed from the pain of death."[38] Aquinas was clear that their penance may still ensure their ultimate salvation, but the Christian community cannot afford the risk that they pose in the world, and therefore capital punishment is appropriate.

Aquinas was able to take this very stark line, as least as it seems to us, through the combination of the history of the theology of heresy with his new psychosomatic rendition of human subjectivity. This provided a potent justification for the prosecution of heretics: their depravity was deeply embodied and therefore hard to eradicate. Aquinas belonged to the Dominicans, the Order of Preachers, an organization founded in 1216 to fight heresy. For the Dominicans, the issue of heresy and its management could never be ignored as it was the basis of their entire institutional mandate. Throughout the thirteenth century, Dominicans became renowned as both theologians and inquisitors. Aquinas was their greatest intellectual, and his scholarly work went some way to defining and maintaining the scare of heresy.

Notes

[25] R. I. Moore, *The Formation of a Persecuting Society* (Oxford: Blackwell, 1987).

[26] On the Council, see Lewis Ayres, *Nicaea and its Legacy* (Oxford: Oxford University Press, 2004).

[27] On heresy and its general context in late antiquity, see *Late Antiquity: A Guide to the Postclassical World*, ed. G. W. Bowersock, Peter Brown, and Oleg Grabar (Cambridge, MA: Belknap, 1989).

[28] On the theology of Lateran IV, see John W. Baldwin, "Paris et Rome en 1215: les réformes du IVe Concile de Latran," *Journal des Savants* 1 (1997): 99–124. See also Clare Monagle, "Theology, Policy and Practice at the Turn of the Thirteenth Century," *Journal of Religious History* 37 (2013): 441–56.

[29] *Decrees of the Ecumenical Councils*, ed. Norman P. Tanner (London: Sheed and Ward, 1990), p. 230.

[30] Tanner, *Decrees*, p. 230.

[31] See Peter Gemeinhardt, "The Trinitarian Theology of Joachim of Fiore," *Archa Verbi* 9 (2012): 9–33.

[32] Tanner, *Decrees*, p. 232.

[33] Tanner, *Decrees*, p. 232.

[34] *Translations and Reprints from the Original Sources of European History*, 6 vols. (Philadelphia: University of Pennsylvania History Department, 1897–1907), 3:12–15.

[35] Norman Tanner, *Ages of Faith: Popular Religion in Late Medieval England and Western Europe* (London: Tauris, 2009), p. 30.

[36] *Summa theologiae* II-II.11.i.iii, p. 114.

[37] *Summa theologiae* II-II.11.iii.co., p. 117.

[38] *Summa theologiae* II-II.11.iv.co., p. 119.

Chapter 3

The Jew

Just as medieval Christian theologians thought through the categories of women and heretics, they also focused upon Jews as a point of difference. The idea of Jewish difference was a crucial category of self-understanding within Christian theology. The history of Christianity as a religion was founded on the moment of separation from Judaism. From the outset, Christianity had negotiated its identity in relation to the Judaism from which it emerged. On the one hand, Christianity superseded Judaism—the revelation of Christ as Messiah completed the prophecies of the Hebrew Bible. Christ repaired the damage that Adam and Eve had done, and rendered null and void the Law that Jews had practised in order to show their respect for God. On the other hand, Christianity only made historical sense if the truth of the Hebrew Bible was respected. Christ's salvific work was only legible if Jewish history was taken into account. Therefore, Christianity was of Judaism and yet repudiated it entirely. Christianity needed Judaism to understand its own foundations, and its own saving work. At the same time, Jews failed to recognize Christ as Messiah, and in so doing had sinned most grievously. The category of the Jew, therefore, presented a challenge to the theologian. It was necessary to find a way to recognize Christianity's Jewish foundations in order to explain just how Christ was able to fulfil the messianic expectation of the Hebrew Bible. Yet, the Jews bore responsibility for Christ's death, in as much as they gave him over to Roman authorities. As such, they were both origin and other to the Christian tradition.[39]

Adam and Eve's sin was necessary for Christian history to begin, as we have seen. This necessity, however, provided no mitigation for their sin. Similarly, Christ needed to be put to death in order to be able to rise from the dead. Christian history is dependent on the crucifixion as the catalyst for the momentous event of the resurrection. The Jews, however, were still to be judged for their failure of recognition, even though their so-called obduracy was in fact enabling for Christian history. In response to this ambivalent status, Augustine of Hippo formulated a doctrine of Jewish witness that obtained well into the Middle Ages. He argued that it was God's will that Jews be tolerated until the end of time, as they provided a living witness to the foundations of Christianity. That is, Jews should be tolerated as their presence bore the truth of Christian teaching. They were a living testament to a dead law, the law that Christian faith made unnecessary. Augustine interpreted Psalm 59:11 as an injunction to protect Jews. The psalm read, "slay them not, lest my people forget: scatter them by thy power." Augustine argued that it was desirable that Jews be protected, and that they be scattered in a diaspora. They had value, but only in relation to Christian self-knowledge.[40]

The status of Jews in Christian communities reflected this. Jewish communities existed, and survived, throughout a number of kingdoms in medieval Europe. Their status was assured through the protection of the monarch. They were outside the normative Christian forms of political identity, wherein an individual's status was granted by participation in either manorial or feudal systems of association. Jews were not peasants, nor were they knights; and obviously, they were not a part of the clergy. They tended to artisanal and mercantile roles. In particular, they often served as moneylenders, as the practice of usury was forbidden to Christians. Christian kings, however, often needed access to funds, and so were dependent upon Jews as a source for loans. Jews occupied a very vulnerable, and highly contingent, position. They could be expelled at any time by the monarch upon whom they relied, often forced to leave their home with great monies owed to them.

During the High Middle Ages, these expulsions increased in number, alongside other forms of persecuting behaviour. Jews were invariably subject to much greater surveillance than their Christian neighbours, usually being required to provide detailed inventories of wealth and assets to their overlords. They were also required, after Lateran IV, to wear identifying markers of their exceptional identity on their person. There are records that in some areas Jews wore the Star of David, in other locations it seems they wore distinct hats.[41] In any case, over the period covered by this book it seems that Jews became particularly visible as a minority in northern Europe, and this visibility was often used in the service of the political agenda of their ostensible protector. It is not surprising that concomitant to this increased visibility, there was a rise in anti-Jewish polemic. Jews became the subject of lurid stories that involved the sacrifice of Christian children. They became increasingly figured as evildoers, with designs on Christian society. Rather than being presented as living witnesses to the law, they became personified as a monstrous other who deserved sanction.

For example, the chronicler Rigord, writing in 1186, set down to explain the events that led to the expulsion of the Jews by Philip Augustus of France in 1182. Rigord explained that the events were prompted because the king had heard

> that the Jews who dwelt in Paris were wont every year on Easter day, or during the sacred week of our Lord's Passion, to go down secretly into underground vaults and kill a Christian as a sort of sacrifice in contempt of the Christian religion.[42]

Rigord then went on to explain how the Jews had used their role as usurers to accumulate vast funds, as well as to trap Christians into servile debt. He reported that some Jewish moneylenders had actually imprisoned Christians in their home when they were unable to pay monies owed. They also employed Christian servants in their apparently lavish estates, thereby putting Christian souls at risk through proximity. What is important here, for our purposes, is the refashioning of the figure of the Jew. Under the doctrine of Jewish witness, the Jew was understood to stand in for a lost past. Increasingly, however, from the twelfth century onwards, the figure of the Jew came to stand for malevolence and threat. As such, it was the self-styled task of the Christian leader to manage this threat. Rigord's chronicle is but one of many, in which we see how this new image of the malevolent and wealthy Jew could be used by leaders to justify persecuting behaviour and practices.

The changes that occurred in relation to the figure of the Jew in western European culture are also visible in the history of theology. As one of the founders of the scholastic project, Peter Lombard was relatively mild about Jews, which is not to say tolerant or supportive. He was interested in Jews in the same way that he was interested in Eve: he wanted to catalogue their sin, and make sense of it in terms of the theology of the will. If the Jews had repudiated Christ, without knowledge of the gravity of their deed, was their sin mitigated at all? That is, how important is intentionality to the assessment of a sinner's sin? By the time of Scotus, however, we see a scholastic theologian making a vigorous case in favour of the forced baptism of Jewish children, against the will of their parents. Lombard considered the history of the Jews as a crucial part of Christian self-knowledge, as a way into his theology of the will. Lombard has nothing to say about real Jews. By the turn of the fourteenth century, however, a scholastic theologian like Scotus has turned his hand to issues that pertain to the status of Jews in their world. The question as to whether or not forced baptism of Jewish children was licit went to the heart of the status of real Jews in the world. Did Jewish parents have parental rights under natural law to educate and nurture their children in the way that they saw fit, or did the imperative to salvation override that right?

Lombard

In Book 1 of the *Sentences* Lombard wrote, paraphrasing Augustine, "God foreknows and foretells even those things which he will not do himself, as he knew and foretold the faithlessness of the Jews, but did not himself cause it."[43] Lombard was moved to ponder this question as part of his larger discussion about the nature of God's will. Each of the gospel narratives of the crucifixion pointed to some level of involvement of Jewish authorities in Christ's death. That is, they point to Jewish leaders bearing a degree of culpability for the execution of the Messiah. Lombard wanted to know if the Jews could, thus, be blamed for Christ's death. The reason being that this question actually pertained to God, rather than the Jews, as Christian theology held that God was all-seeing and all-knowing. God was past, present, and future, and yet outside of time altogether. God's greatness meant that the Jewish authorities could not have betrayed Christ without it being willed to some degree by God. Surely the Jewish leaders who gave Christ to Pilate should be understood as performing God's will. God sent down his son precisely to perform this saving work, which could not occur without his death.

Just as we saw in the discussion of Eve, the contrast between human sin and God's omnipotence was the place where Lombard negotiated his understanding of the human will. God can, and does, will whatever he pleases. That is his prerogative. At the same time, however, humans must have free will in order to choose God properly. This is an irreducible contradiction, one that cannot entirely be resolved. Lombard's solution was to say that when God willed the crucifixion he willed good, because he understood the transformative nature of the event. He willed a bad thing with good intention, and for a good end. The Jews, on the other hand, willed impiously,

> That God's good will is fulfilled by the evil wills of men, as happened in Christ's passion, where something was done which God willed by a good will and the Jews by an evil one; and yet they willed something which God did not will [...] God willed [Christ] to die by a good will, but the Jews crucified him by an impious will. And the Jews willed by an evil will something that God willed by a good will, namely that Christ should suffer and die; yet they willed something else which God did not will, namely to kill Christ, which was an evil action and a sin. For God did not will the action of the Jews, but he willed

the passion of Christ [...] Indeed, the whole Trinity willed that Christ suffer, yet it did not will that the Jews kill: because the Trinity willed the suffering of Christ, but did not will the guilt of the Jews; yet it was not unwilling that it happened: for if God had been unwilling, it would not have happened.[44]

I have quoted this passage so that we can gauge the problematic logic at play. Lombard is emphatic that the Jews be culpable, even when this argument is unnecessary theologically. In fact, both Anselm and Abelard had assessed the situation differently in the century prior to the production of the *Sentences*. Those theologians had both canvassed the possibility that the Jews could not be held to account for Christ's death, in as much as they did not will the death of the Messiah. Without intentionality, as they expressed it, it was not a sin. In order to argue for Jewish guilt, Lombard must assert the primacy of man's free will as a measure of sin, rather than for intentionality, even when this argument threatens to destabilize God's all-knowing sovereignty.

Around the same time as Lombard was writing his *Sentences*, another Peter was composing an anti-Jewish polemic. Peter the Venerable was one of the most important figures in Christendom, abbot of the powerful monastery at Cluny. He had the ear of the most influential people in Christendom, including popes and monarchs. Where Peter Lombard was interested in the historical Jew as a way into Christian theological debates, Peter the Venerable was interested in contemporary Jews, the threat that they posed, as well as the possibility that they could be converted. Peter the Venerable was not a scholastic theologian, and it is not my intention to read him as such. Rather, in the words of Peter the Venerable we see a departure from the aforementioned doctrine of Jewish witness. This doctrine, based in the theology of Augustine, had urged the protection of Jews as they provided testimony to the pre-history of Christianity. Peter the Venerable, however, wrote a polemic against the Jews of his time, addressing them directly, and deploying a combination of pleas and fetid insults to encourage their conversion. If we are to understand the status of Jews in Christendom, which was to alter significantly over the coming century, we need to hear voices such as Peter the Venerable. For example, he wrote

> Acknowledge that the cause of your very harsh condemnation is this: that you did not recognize, did not receive, did not worship the messiah once he came, the one that for such a long time you sang, read, and preached would come, but instead you spurned him, mocked him, slew him, in your detestable fashion.[45]

This is a small snippet of Peter the Venerable's work, one that has much nastier things to say. It goes some way, I hope, to show the stakes of the theology of the Jews as killers of Christ. Even though Lombard speaks of Jews without invective, and renders them in the past rather than the present, he insists without hesitation that their weak wills lead to Christ's death. Lombard refuses mitigation, even when his theology of God's will might permit a softening of judgement upon Jewish culpability. The stakes of this position are placed in sharp relief, when read alongside the intervention of Peter the Venerable.

Scotus

In spite of growing enmity towards Jews across Christendom a consensus remained among theologians that Jews should not be forcibly converted, and that a true conversion could only take place in the presence of free will. Aquinas, in particular, argued forcibly against the forced conversion of Jewish children. His argument was two-fold. He considered that one could not consent adequately without reason, and that reason only occurred in the mature individual. It was important for the integrity of faith that if unbelievers were to come to belief and to seek to join the Church that their conversion be full and complete. The baptism of infants born to Christian parents was a different issue, because those children could be nurtured in the Church, and so the risk of their apostasy was very low. In relation to Jewish children, however, who were baptized against the wishes of their parents, there was a very real risk of a return to the faith of the parents. This would not only be detrimental to their soul but dangerous to the Christian community to have their own moving between these worlds. The other aspect of Aquinas's argument against the forcible baptism of Jewish children was that to do so would be to violate the natural rights of the parents. Aquinas wrote:

> For a child is by nature part of its father: thus, at first, it is not distinct from his parents as to its body, so long as it is enfolded within its mother's womb, and later on after birth, and before it has the use of its free-will, it is enfolded in the care of its parents, which is like a spiritual womb [...] Hence it would be contrary to natural justice, if a child, before coming to the use of reason, were to be taken away from its parents' custody, or anything done to it against its parents' wish.[46]

Here, Aquinas declared that Jews' status as exceptional within Christendom did not mean that they should not be granted natural justice. In fact Aquinas is explicit on this matter, he acknowledges that Jews are "bondsmen of princes by civil bondage,"[47] but insists that this does not exclude the operations of divine and natural law. None of this is to say that Aquinas is supportive of Jews in a general sense, or radical in his treatment of Jews in the remainder of his theology. Rather, it is important to note that there was the capacity within the contours of what I am calling the scholastic project to find arguments that recognized forms of human dignity outside of Christianity.

Scotus took a very different perspective on this issue. Firstly, he argued that consent, normatively understood, was not strictly necessary to achieve a satisfactory baptism. Innocent III had argued in 1201 that a forcible baptism could be licit if the person being baptized ceased to protest during the baptism. That is, he argued that the absence of protest could constitute assent. Scotus, writing one hundred years or so later, wrote that "if someone does not consent, but only by not wanting, I say that he receives the sacrament if he consents virtually."[48] He argued that because the human will was timid and frail, it was almost impossible for a human to will fully. God understands this limitation, Scotus argued, and so he was still able to confer the privilege of baptism, even upon an ostensible non-believer. As to the issue of whether or not Jewish children should be baptized against the wishes of their parents, Scotus also departed from Aquinas's position. Where Aquinas had argued that Jews were still protected by natural law, even if they were bonded to the sovereign as their protector, Scotus turned this position on its head, suggesting that while a normal Christian could not perform a baptism on a Jewish child against the parents' wishes, a prince could. He argued that the role of the prince was to function as an intermediary between God and man, therefore the prince needed to do God's work in the world. Since the Jews were under his care and protection, the best he could do for them was bring them into the community of the faithful. Scotus wrote:

> Above all the Prince is obliged to further the service of God. It is therefore necessary that he should withdraw minors from parental power, if the parents want to educate them otherwise than in the service of God. For God is the highest and most elevated Lord. Hence the prince has to bring those little children to divine worship.[49]

Scotus's theology posited a different notion of the monarch's work in the world than that which had obtained in medieval thought beforehand. The king had been understood to rule with the consent of the Church, and to be ultimately responsible to the papacy. Of course this was not always, and mostly was not, the case in practice. It was the agreed upon political theology, however, that the papacy had intercessory powers, and it was the papacy alone that could anoint a secular leader. Scotus, however, was articulating a transformative political theology that assigned a dynamic theological legitimacy to the sovereign, a legitimacy that would eventually be understood as constituting a divine right. The rights and duty of the sovereign, at least when it came to forcible baptism of Jews, trumped the natural rights of Jewish subjects. The sovereign was above the law because they embodied a higher form of the law.

And what of the doctrine of the Jewish witness that had been so central to the status of Jews within Christendom? If forcible conversion was the duty of the sovereign, what then of the need that Jews remain in Christendom as a reminder of the law, as a container for Christian memory of the old dispensation? In answer to this question, Scotus developed a response described by Nancy Turner as one of "almost breathtaking literalism."[50] He suggested that a small number of Jews should be isolated upon an island somewhere, and be permitted to practise their religion there. The remainder, however, should be converted. In short, Scotus suggested that a limited number of Jews should be ghettoized for the spiritual comfort of Christian populations, while the rest should be forced into the Christian community. There are many theories as to why Scotus's theology of conversion took on such an intolerant line. Some argue that over the course of the thirteenth century, Christian elites had come to an understanding of the Talmud. Consequently, they realized that Judaism was not an ossified religion that bore witness only to the time of Christ, but in fact had a dynamic textual and liturgical history. Therefore, Jews could no longer bear witness to the past in the manner that had been assumed. More broadly, as Christendom became defined over the thirteenth century, and as its theological borders were policed via the inquisition, Christian society seems to have become more alarmed by difference and more fearful of contamination.

From Lombard to Scotus we see a significant change in the use of the Jew in theology. For Lombard the Jew was what Jeremy Cohen has called the "hermeneutic Jew."[51] Lombard seems concerned with Jews as a limit concept, as he had been with Eve as well. The woman and the Jew, both of whom must be *a priori* understood as having a deformed will, provide an argumentative bedrock against which theology can be built. Something entirely different seems to be going on with Duns Scotus, who is offering theological justifications for a policy shift that moves from tolerance to terror. Scotus, of course, does not speak for all scholastic theologians of the period. In fact, in many of his positions he was conceptually avant-garde. His theology of the Jews, however, does show scholastic theology in its most reactionary mode, collaborating ideologically with the persecuting society.

Notes

[39] See Jeremy Cohen's *Living Letters of the Law: Ideas of the Jew in Medieval Christianity* (Berkeley: University of California Press, 1999), and Irven Resnick, *Marks of Distinction: Christian Perceptions of Jews in the High Middle Ages* (Washington, DC: Catholic University of America Press, 2012).

[40] See Paula Fredriksen, *Augustine and the Jews: A Christian Defense of Jews and Judaism* (New York: Doubleday, 2008).

[41] For background, see Robert Chazan, *The Jews of Medieval Western Christendom* (Cambridge: Cambridge University Press, 2006).

[42] *Oeuvres de Rigord et de Guillaume le Breton, historiens de Philippe-Auguste*, ed. H. F. Delaborde, 2 vols. (Paris: Société de l'Histoire de France, 1882–85), 1:146–49.

[43] Peter Lombard, *The Sentences* 1.38.1, trans. Giulio Silano as *The Sentences Book 1: The Mystery of The Trinity* (Toronto: Pontifical Institute of Mediaeval Studies, 2007), p. 215.

[44] Lombard, *The Sentences* 1.48.2.1, pp. 259–60.

[45] Peter the Venerable, *Against the Inveterate Obduracy of the Jews*, trans. Irven Resnick (Washington, DC: Catholic University of America Press, 2013), p. 50.

[46] *Summa theologiae* II-II.10.xii.co., pp. 111–12.

[47] *Summa theologiae* II-II.10.xii.iii, p. 112.

[48] The following quotatin from Scotus is taken from Nancy L. Turner's excellent article, "Jewish Witness, Forced Confession and Island Living: John Duns Scotus on Jews and Judaism," in *Christian Attitudes towards the Jews in the Middle Ages: A Casebook*, ed. Michael Frassetto (New York: Routledge, 2007), pp. 183–209 at 195.

[49] Henri A. Krop, "Duns Scotus and the Jews: Scholastic Theology and Enforced Conversion in the Thirteenth Century," *Nederlands archief voor kerkgeschiedenis/Dutch Review of Church History* 69 (1989): 161–75 at 165.

[50] Turner, "Jewish Witness," p. 198.

[51] Cohen, *Living Letters of the Law*, pp. 2–4.

Conclusion

When I teach medieval theology to students, many of whom have little theological knowledge or experience of religion, they often look at me incredulously. They cannot believe that people believed. They are surprised by the intensity of theological speculation during the Middle Ages, and the evidence that an entire intellectual system was produced around faith in the fundamental event of Christ's resurrection. They are often particularly shocked to find out that the foundations of the university as an institution, the very institution in which we have our lessons, lay in the teaching of Christian theology. They think of the university as a place of science and of reason, as a place in which they learn about the world and try to think uncompromisingly about the truth. I explain to them that medieval theologians also thought that the university was a place for confrontation with the truth, informed by principles of science and reason. They used the word *scientia*, but for them it meant knowledge. They used the word *ratio*, and for them it meant the rational order of things through which God had informed and made the world. My point to the students is that medieval scholars believed in their intellectual protocols, and had faith that they were producing knowledge that was real and truthful.

It is, I think, an important lesson for anyone to learn, that communities build the world around them based on shared beliefs, and develop systems of meaning that fortify and nurture those beliefs. Culture is to some degree a feedback loop in which mutually constitutive messages buttress one another to build consensus. In my teaching I ask the students to think about what unspoken, and shared, assumptions underlie our conversation in the classroom. What is the unsaid mutuality that enables us to sit in the same room and talk to each other? This is a denaturalizing moment. We try to work out what is hiding in plain sight, what are the shared assumptions about knowledge and identity that enable us to communicate at that moment. What, in short, is our faith that generates our inquiry? Often, the answer is that as a collective we are invested in a fuzzy secular humanism. In thinking about what went without saying in the Middle Ages, I want my students to ask themselves what goes without saying in their own world.

To make sense of scholastic theology, then, we need to give it the benefit of the doubt. This is not the same as letting it off the hook. I have spent this book cataloguing this theology as a place of exclusions, that builds Christian identity on the back of the production of an other. My purpose is certainly not to be an apologist for scholasticism. But having mapped the scholastic project, I am keen also to place the powerful caveat that our own moral judgements upon the project ought not preclude a thoughtful engagement with its history.

Scholastic theology emerged through practices of teaching, of argumentation and controversy. It has a history, one that is intimately linked to the history of privilege, power, and authority in the Middle Ages. This theology may seem, to the modern observer, to be obscurantist and technical. It presents a great many challenges to the reader, and can feel forbidding and confusing. For the twenty-first-century student attempting to come to grips with the medieval world of western Europe, other texts seem to permit much greater access to the culture of that time and place. For example, a chivalric romance or an altarpiece might seem more alive to our eyes and ears, more engaging and proximate. I want to argue in this book, however, that the student (or, indeed, the scholar) ought not avoid theology for fear of its erudition and abstraction. Rather, as I hope I have shown, scholastic theology offers an important site of ideological contestation and negotiation, in which we can see core issues of the time playing out. That is, scholastic theologians were world builders. They constructed an entire system of teachings, all of which hung together within their logical frames. To understand medieval culture, in both its most hegemonic and transgressive modes, we must come to grips with the dominant theological architecture of the time.

Further Reading

Here are some suggestions for further reading in the field, in addition to the works already cited in the volume's notes.

Abulafia, Anna Sapir. *Christian-Jewish Relations 1000–1300: Jews in the Service of Medieval Christendom*. Abingdon: Routledge, 2011.
Analyses theological, socio-economic, and political services Jews were required to render to medieval Christendom. The nature of Jewish service varied greatly as Christian rulers struggled to reconcile the desire to profit from the presence of Jewish men and women in their lands with conflicting theological notions about Judaism. Jews meanwhile had to deal with the many competing authorities and interests in the localities in which they lived; their continued presence hinged on a fine balance between theology and pragmatism. This book examines the impact of the Crusades on Christian–Jewish relations and how anti-Jewish libels were used to define relations. It draws on Hebrew and Latin liturgical and exegetical material, and narrative, polemical, and legal sources.

Cohen, Mark. *Under Crescent and Cross: The Jews in the Middle Ages*. Princeton: Princeton University Press, 1994.

A systematic comparison of Jewish life in medieval Islam and Christendom, and the first in-depth explanation of why medieval Islamic–Jewish relations, though not utopic, were less confrontational and violent than those between Christians and Jews in the West.

Colish, Marcia. *Medieval Foundations of the Western Intellectual Tradition*. New Haven: Yale, 1999.

An analysis of the course of Western intellectual history between AD 400 and 1400, divided into two parts: the first surveying the comparative modes of thought and varying success of Byzantine, Latin-Christian, and Muslim cultures; the second taking readers from the eleventh-century revival of learning to the period in which the vibrancy of Western intellectual culture enabled it to stamp its imprint well beyond the frontiers of Christendom.

Courtenay, William J. *Parisian Scholars in the Early Fourteenth Century: A Social Portrait*. Cambridge: Cambridge University Press, 1999.

A study of the social, geographical, and disciplinary composition of the scholarly community at Paris, based on the financial record of tax levied on university members in the academic year 1329–30. Containing the names, financial level, and often addresses of the majority of the masters and most prominent students, it is a singularly rich source for the social history of a medieval university. It offers a thorough examination of the financial account, the history of such collections, and the case (a rape by a student) that precipitated legal expenses and the need for a collection. The book explores residential patterns, the relationship of students, masters, and tutors, social class and levels of wealth, interaction with the royal court, and the geographical background of university scholars.

Elliott, Dyan. *Proving Woman: Female Mysticism and Inquisitional Practice in Late Medieval Europe.* Princeton: Princeton University Press, 2004.

Around 1215, female mystics and their sacramental devotion were among orthodoxy's most sophisticated weapons in the fight against heresy. Holy women's claims to be in direct communication with God placed them in positions of unprecedented influence. Yet by the end of the Middle Ages female mystics were frequently mistrusted, derided, and in fear of their lives. It shows medieval society's progressive reliance on the inquisitional procedure. Inquisition was soon used for resolving most questions of proof. It was employed for distinguishing saints and heretics; it underwrote the new emphasis on confession in both sacramental and judicial spheres; and it heralded the reintroduction of torture as a mechanism for extracting proof through confession. Witch hunts were just around the corner.

Evans, G. R. *The Medieval Theologians: An Introduction to Theology in the Medieval Period.* Oxford: Wiley-Blackwell, 2001.

A clear and comprehensive introduction to the period from the fifth to sixteenth centuries through an examination of the key individual theologians of the time. Chronologically arranged, it allows readers to trace developments in the field by individual theologian, rather than by theme.

Gender and Christianity in Medieval Europe: New Perspectives.
Edited by Lisa Bitel and Felice Lifshitz. Philadelphia: University
of Pennsylvania Press, 2008.

Six historians explore how medieval people professed
Christianity, how they performed gender, and how the
two coincided. Daily religious decisions people made were
influenced by gender roles: women's pious donations, for
instance, were limited by laws of inheritance and marriage
customs; male clerics' behaviour depended upon their
understanding of masculinity as much as on the demands
of liturgy. The job of religious practitioner, whether as a
nun, monk, priest, bishop, or some less formal participant,
involved not only professing a set of religious ideals but
also professing gender in both ideal and practical terms.
The scholars also argue that medieval Europeans chose
how to be women or men (or some complex combination
of the two), just as they decided whether and how to be
religious. In this sense, religious institutions freed men
and women from some of the gendered limits otherwise
imposed by society.

Jordan, William Chester. *The French Monarch and the Jews: From
Philip Augustus to the Last Capetians.* Philadelphia: University
of Pennsylvania Press, 1989.

Assesses the relationship between "Jewish policy" and
the development of royal institutions and ideology in the
period during which the foundations of the French state
were being laid. Royal policy under Philip Augustus was
erratic. Official efforts to humiliate the Jews and ruin their
businesses alternated with attempts to provide a climate
that encouraged their business while at the same time
imposing economic and social disabilities that made other
aspects of their lives intolerable. Louis IX, on the other
hand, was single-minded in his efforts to induce the Jews
to convert. Under Philip the Fair, the Jews were expelled

and their property confiscated to the financial benefit of the crown. This work shows the effects of the expulsion of the Jews, especially during the first years of their exile to the principalities bordering the French king's domain.

Mews, Constant. *Abelard and Heloise: Great Medieval Thinkers*. Oxford: Oxford University Press, 2005.

A brief, accessible introduction to the lives and thought of two of the most controversial personalities of the Middle Ages. This book attempts to place them properly in the context of twelfth-century thought.

Moore, R. I. *The First European Revolution c. 970–1215*. Oxford: Blackwell, 2000.

A radical reassessment of Europe from the late tenth to the early thirteenth centuries, drawing on insights from social anthropology and other periods and places. The author's earlier works on heresy, dissent, and a persecuting society are foundational for this period.

Nirenberg, David. *Anti-Judaism: The Western Tradition*. New York City: Norton, 2014.

Argues that anti-Judaism is a central way of thinking in the Western tradition. Questions of how we are Jewish and, more critically, how and why we are not have been churning within the Western imagination throughout its history. Ancient Egyptians, Greeks, and Romans; Christians and Muslims of every period; even modern secularists have used Judaism in constructing their visions of the world. The thrust of this tradition construes Judaism as an opposition, a danger often from within, to be criticized, attacked, and eliminated. The intersections of these ideas with the Roman destruction of the Second Temple, the Spanish Inquisition, and the German Holocaust are well known.

The Oxford Handbook of Women and Gender in Medieval Europe. Edited by Ruth Mazo Karras and Judith Bennett. Oxford: Oxford University Press, 2013.

> Thirty-seven essays by prominent scholars address interpretive challenges common to all fields of women's and gender history—that is, how best to uncover the experiences of ordinary people from archives formed mainly by and about elite males, and how to combine social histories of lived experiences with cultural histories of gendered discourses and identities.

Pegg, Mark. *A Most Holy War: The Albigensian Crusade and the Battle for Christendom.* New York: Oxford University Press, 2007.

> In January 1208, a papal legate was murdered in southern France. Pope Innocent III accused heretics of the crime and called upon all Christians to exterminate heresy in Languedoc in a great crusade. This most holy war, the first in which Christians were promised salvation for killing other Christians, lasted twenty bloody years. But the author argues that the Cathars never existed. The struggle to cleanse the world of heresy, with millennial fervour, led to the creation of the Inquisition, the rise of anti-Semitism, and holy violence of the Reconquista in Spain and then the New World.

The Postcolonial Middle Ages. Edited by Jeffrey Jerome Cohen. Palgrave: New York, 2000.

> This collection of fourteen essays is the first to apply post-colonial theory to the Middle Ages, and to critique that theory through the excavation of a distant past. The essays examine the establishment of colony, empire, and nationalism in order to expose the mechanisms of oppression through which "aboriginal," "native," or simply pre-existent cultures are displaced, eradicated, or transformed.

Southern, R. W. *Scholastic Humanism and the Unification of Europe*, Vol. 1: *Foundations*. Oxford: Blackwell, 1995; Vol. 2: *The Heroic Ages*. Oxford: Blackwell, 2001.

Authoritative presentation of how a group of scholars, mainly centred on Paris and Bologna, began an enterprise of unprecedented scope. Their intention was to produce a once-and-for-all body of knowledge that would be as perfect as humanity's fallen state permits, and which would provide a view of God, nature, and human conduct, promoting order in this world and blessedness in the next. Covering the mid-eleventh to early thirteenth centuries, these two volumes describe the creative intellectual impulse that brought it into being and sustained it, and show how it was able to bring into existence a systematic body of knowledge of the natural and supernatural worlds, including the whole area of human relations, which together embraced all areas of possible truth and defined the conduct required of all members of western Christendom.

Illustrations

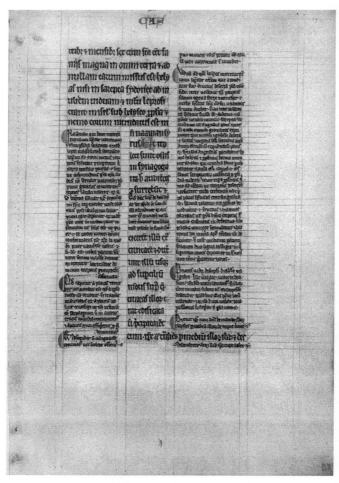

Figure 1. Luke 4:25–31 with Glossa ordinaria, *France, ca. 1200.*

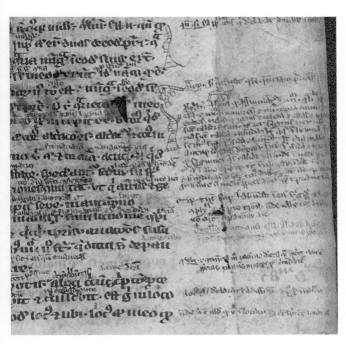

Figure 2. Detail of Liber sex principiorum, *France, ca. 1175–1250.*

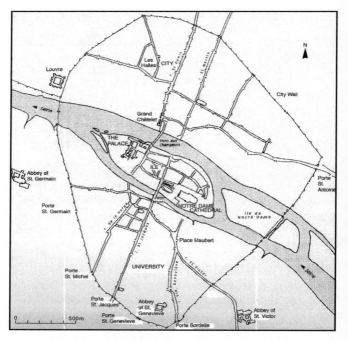

Map 1. Paris ca. 1200 showing main university sites and religious houses.

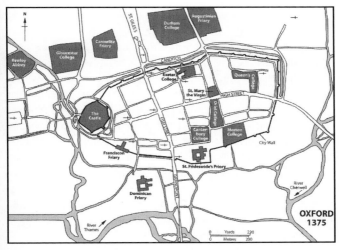

Map 2. Oxford ca. 1375 showing the location of contemporary university buildings and other centres of learning.

Comments on Illustrations

Figure 1. The scholastics were invested in a program of careful, close reading of authoritative texts, beginning with the bible, and created manuscripts that reflected these aims. The main text would be presented in large, formal, widely spaced script, surrounded by a sea of smaller commentary. At the top of the page, running titles—here "Luke chapter four" (*iiii [Lu]cas*), stretched across this page and the one preceding—allowed readers to quickly navigate between widely separated parts of the book, facilitating comparison and analysis between passages. Ancestors of the modern paraph mark (¶) further divide the commentary into paragraphs. Luke 4:25–31 with *Glossa ordinaria*, France, ca. 1200. (Photo: Kalamazoo, Western Michigan University, Dwight B. Waldo Library MS 141 recto.)

Figure 2. Scholastic bookmaking practices are the forerunners of many features of modern books, such as alphabetical indexes, cross-references, or, as here, academic footnotes. Brief, sometimes one-word quotations from the main text, paired symbols, or even stylized drawings of pointing hands (*maniculae*, literally "little hands") helped readers to locate the word or phrase that prompted a marginal note. The annotator of this text, itself a commentary on Aristotle's *Categories*, has employed all three of these reference techniques. Detail of *Liber sex principiorum*, France, ca. 1175–1250. (Photo: Kalamazoo, Western Michigan University, Dwight B. Waldo Library MS 148 recto.)

additional permission and further information contact the WMU Libraries, Special Collections and Rare Book Department: lib-rbr@wmich.edu.

Map 1. Paris ca. 1200 showing main university sites and religious houses. (After Richard H. Rouse and Mary A. Rouse, *Manuscripts and their Makers: Commercial Book Producers in Medieval Paris 1200-1500*, vol. 1 [Harvey Miller Publishers, 2000], p. 414.)

Map 2. Oxford ca. 1375 showing the location of contemporary university buildings and other centres of learning. (After Eleanor Chance et al., "Medieval Oxford," in *A History of the County of Oxford*, vol. 4, *The City of Oxford*, ed. Alan Crossley and C. R. Elrington [London: Victoria County History, 1979], http://www.british-history.ac.uk/vch/oxon/vol4/pp3-73.)

Printed and bound by CPI Group (UK) Ltd, Croydon, CR0 4YY

13/06/2024

14514600-0001